GETTING HIGH
IN NATURAL WAYS

"A wealth of fascinating and useful information, engagingly written and clearly communicated. Should be required reading for junior high and high school curricula."

JONATHAN S. KELLERMAN, Ph.D.
Clinical Associate Professor of Pediatrics,
USC School of Medicine
Author, *Helping The Fearful Child*

"The book is wonderful!

I began reading it from the perspective of an adult evaluating reading material for teenagers, but quickly found myself doing the excercises. What seemed important to me was that the authors point out how simple it is to feel good and how little we realize this. GETTING HIGH gives the reader permission to laugh and cry and play.

I will see to it that our counselors and human relations teachers have access to GETTING HIGH IN NATURAL WAYS."

ROBERTA DRAKE, High School Counselor
Chaffey Joint Union High School District,
Ontario, California

"I found the book very positive — just reading it made me feel good. The section on the brain was so understandable; though a complicated subject it was made very simple. The chapter on crying made me want to ask a man, 'Why don't you cry to express your feelings?', or 'Do you?' 'Reaching In, Reaching Out' and 'Love' gave me lots to think about. Most teens do not wish to be preached to because it turns us off. But I felt the authors explained things so that we would be encouraged to try them on our own."

HEIDI SONZENA, High School senior,
Co-author, *Raising Each Other:
An INFOBOOK for Parents and Teens*

ABOUT THE AUTHORS

Nancy Levinson is the author of nine books for children and young adults, as well as numerous stories and articles. Her most recent book is *The Ruthie Greene Show,* a comic novel for teens. Formerly a teacher in the Head Start program, she is often in classrooms at all grade levels, talking about the joys of reading and its relationship to writing.

Born in Minneapolis, Ms. Levinson now lives in Beverly Hills, California. She has two teenage sons, who not only let her use their computer but provide free editorial advice. She is a member of the Society of Children's Book Writers and of the Southern California Council on Literature for Children and Young People.

Joanne Rocklin holds a Ph.D. in clinical psychology and works with children, adolescents, adults, and families at the Burbank Child Guidance Clinic and the Omega Center for Mental Health in Woodland Hills. She lectures frequently on issues of child development and parenting, the importance of early reading, learning disabilities, and drug abuse. She has also published a first novel, a humorous children's story entitled *Sonia Begonia* which appeared in 1985.

Originally from Montreal, she now lives in Los Angeles with her two sons. She is a member of the American, the California, and the Los Angeles Psychological Associations, the Society of Children's Book Writers, and Independent Writers of Southern California.

Levinson and Rocklin met in a writing class and discovered they enjoyed writing and working together. They have given joint workshops on reading and the very young child, and produced booklists to assist parents in selecting reading materials for children. This is their first book together.

GETTING HIGH IN NATURAL WAYS

An Infobook
for
Young People
of All Ages

**Nancy Levinson
and Joanne Rocklin, Ph.D.**

Hunter
House

The universe is change,

our life is what our thoughts make it.

— Marcus Aurelius

    Hunter House Inc., Publishers
    P.O. Box 1302
    Claremont CA 91711

Library of Congress Cataloging-in-Publication Data

Levinson, Nancy Smiler.
    Getting high in natural ways

       1. Youth — United States.   2. Adolescent psychology.
3. Youth — United States — Recreation — Psychological aspects.
4. Happiness.   I. Rocklin, Joanne.   II. Title.
HQ796.L398   1986   305.2'35   85-14458
ISBN 0-89793-036-3

Cover design by Qalagraphia
Cover painting by Luis Caughman, line art by Paul Frindt
Set in 11/13 Palatino by Highpoint Type & Graphics, with titles in
Avant Garde Demi
Printed by Delta Lithograph Co., Van Nuys, California

Manufactured in the United States of America

9 8 7 6 5 4 3 2 1   First edition

CONTENTS

INTRO-DUCTION

You feel great; you feel like singing at the top of your lungs, and you don't care who is around.

Maybe you've won a race

or aced an exam

or had your first kiss

or maybe you're happy for no reason at all.

Whatever it is, don't you wish you could hold on to that feeling forever? You can't keep it forever, of course, but you certainly can make it last longer or recapture it again and again.

Scientists today are making exciting discoveries about the connections between feelings, thoughts, and the central nervous system. With this new understanding about how the mind and body influence each other, we now realize that we have the power to achieve "natural highs."

Some people take drugs to get high. Chemical highs make them feel good at first, but after a while they become dependent on drugs just to feel normal. They may feel ill when they stop using drugs, so they believe they have no choice but to continue using them. In contrast, you can get naturally high again and again without "overdosing." You have the power to choose.

Quite often we are not fully tuned in to our emotions or what is really happening at that moment when we experience an extra-special feeling. There are many everyday, pleasure-filled experiences that we take for granted. By giving more thought to these experiences you may be able to do terrific things for yourself. As you become more aware of and sensitive to what turns you on, you may be able to discover new, natural ways to get high.

Searching for new ways to feel good does not mean you will always be able to do away with pain and sorrow. Life is not like that. Plans don't always work. Dreams don't always come true. Accidents happen. We all have to do things we don't like doing and face unpleasant moments. But these are balanced by those special moments in life when we feel good, really good.

The following chapters explore a variety of natural ways to feel good. There are the popular physical activities such as running, dancing, and exercising. But there are also ways to achieve highs, such as being at peace with oneself, feeling love, or enjoying a sense of accomplishment. And there are some ways to feel good that we don't often think about.

As you read about all of them, think about your own life and the many ways in which you can help yourself to feel good, lift your spirits when you're down, and enjoy life to the fullest.

You can make it happen.

1

VOODOO
AND THE BRAIN

Feeling good is a process involving both the mind and the body. In order to understand this, let's take a quick look at how the brain works.

Your brain is really a chemical machine.

Modern medicine, using the most highly developed technological equipment, is confirming what humans have suspected throughout centuries: namely, that the interconnection between mind and body is powerful. Scientific research tells us that what we think and what we do affect the brain and its chemistry. The chemical changes in the brain, in turn, create a feedback system which influences our emotions and behavior.

Imagine these scenes:

— A victim of voodoo magic is hearing ominous chants, smelling strange scents. No one actually touches him, but he falls to the ground with terrible cramps and dies a horrid death.

— The members of your chemistry class are selected to participate in a research experiment. Just before a tough exam, the class is given a pill and told that it will calm the nerves. One half receives a real relaxant, the other half of the class is given a similar pill containing only sugar. No one knows which pill he or she has received. When the results are tabulated, it is found that the students given the real pill did relax, but so did those who swallowed the "fake" sugar pill. How could a mere sugar pill cause this to happen?

— On an Olympic field, a tense, competing athlete prays for extra strength and stamina. He begins to feel a calming of his nerves, his tension subsides, and a surge of courage courses through his blood. With renewed energy he goes on.

These three scenarios, which will be discussed again later, are revealing examples of the mind's effect on the body. In each case the bodily reactions are based on some emotion or belief; today, the effects of those beliefs can be understood better by taking into account the power of brain chemistry.

THE NERVOUS SYSTEM

A brief explanation of the body's nervous system will help clarify the relationship between your moods, thoughts, and bodily reactions.

The Neuron

The nervous system is a network of **neurons** (nerve cells) leading from the brain and contacting every part of the human body. Messages are carried to and from the brain by means of this system. Neurons are different from all other cells in the body. Other cells, such as fat or muscle cells, can only receive information. Neurons, however, are also able to store and transmit information to other neurons, muscles, or glands.

The different parts of a typical neuron are shown in the illustration below.

The **dendrite** is the branch of the nerve cell that receives information from the skin or other neurons. The **axon** is the branch of the neuron that transmits information. The **cell body** is located between the dendrite and the axon and provides nourishment for the entire nerve cell. Depending on their function, the neurons of the human nervous system have a variety of shapes and sizes. **Motor neurons,** like the one in the illustration, carry messages from the spinal cord to the muscles or glands, and have very long axons, because of the relatively long route they must travel.

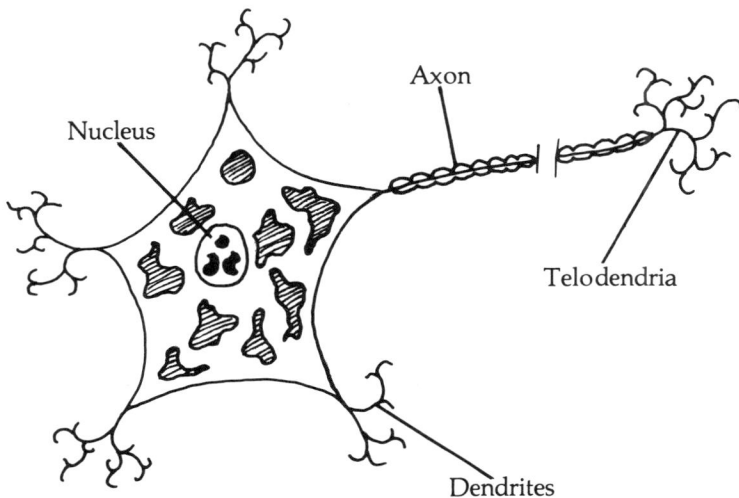

A TYPICAL MOTOR NEURON

Sensory neurons carry incoming messages from the skin to the spinal cord. The dendrites of the sensory neurons have specialized receptors to receive information from the skin. Neurons whose function it is to receive information from other neurons are called **interneurons,** and usually have many dendrites.

Our Two Nervous Systems
The nervous system is divided into two major parts: the central nervous system and the peripheral nervous system.

The Central Nervous System is composed of all the neurons and nerve tracts of the brain and spinal cord. The brain is the master controller of this system, and the spinal cord connects the brain with the rest of the body.

The Peripheral Nervous System consists of the nerve fibers outside the brain and spinal cord, in the limbs and trunk of your body. It also includes:
The autonomic nervous system, which is the part of the nervous system that rules over the involuntary functions of your body (the functions that you usually cannot consciously control, such as heart rate and perspiration.) The autonomic nervous system, in turn, has two major parts:
The sympathetic system. This plays a role in preparing your body for action in response to emotion or stress. (For example, when you are frightened or angry or feeling "up," your heart rate and blood pressure increase.)
The parasympathetic system. This helps your body and its functions return to and maintain a relaxed state after the emotion or stress have passed.

Let us look at how these different parts work together. Whenever you do something or react to something, messages are transmitted between neurons of the central and peripheral nervous systems by way of special chemicals called **neurotransmitters.** In the picture of a neuron you see that at the end of nerve cell axons are tiny hairlike extensions called **telodendria.** Telodendria secrete neurotranmitters which act on the dendrites or cell bodies of other neurons. As you read this sentence, or when you pick up a pencil or sip a soda — whenever you speak or think or do anything — different neurotransmitters are being secreted and are affecting various areas of the brain. About two dozen neurotransmitters have been discovered in the last decade, and scientists believe there may be as many as two hundred more whose functions are yet to be found.

Let's return to the three scenes described at the beginning of this chapter to understand more clearly the power of these chemicals.

Our poor voodoo victim had a strong belief in voodoo magic — the idea that the death or illness of an enemy can be "willed" by a powerful person. This overwhelming anxiety resulted in a stimulation of part of his brain called the **hypothalamus.** The hypothalamus triggered his sympathetic system to prepare for action, which greatly increased the release of the neurotransmitter **norepinephrine** by certain neurons in the brain.

Immediately he started to sweat. His blood pressure rose. His heart began to quiver madly. As a result, his heart could no longer pump and circulate blood throughout his body. What he died of was cardiac arrest!

Tests have shown that norepinephrine is a very powerful neurotransmitter. Depending on which neuron pathways are operating, the release of this substance is probably also involved with feelings of excitement, euphoria, and alertness, as well as with anxiety. Other known neurotransmitters are:

Acetycholine, which is involved in memory, sleep, and the action of the autonomic nervous system.

Serotonin. Studies have shown that this neurotransmitter is probably involved in pain regulation, sleep, and sex.

Endorphins. These newly discovered neurotransmitters are understood to relieve pain, improve mood, and give us a general sense of well-being.

When subjects believe that they have taken a pill that will put them to sleep, a chemical response transmitting sleep messages is triggered. Those who have been in pain and belive that they have taken a painkiller *do* feel marked relief. Are their thoughts and hopes releasing endorphins or other yet-to-be-discovered neurotransmitters? It seems that the answer is yes.

It is not surprising, then, that the students who believed that something was going to tranquilize them actually did relax. That is called the **placebo effect.**

Chances are that the athlete's prayers triggered a complex interplay of neurotransmitters, too. His nerves were calmed. His alertness was increased, and so were his feelings of strength.

Knowledge of the brain's chemistry has allowed scientists to learn more about the way neurotransmitters behave in mentally ill people. It is thought that neurotransmitters are involved in causing schizophrenia and depression. Scientists are learning how to use drugs to alleviate these illnesses, when the brain's chemical system goes awry and the individual cannot function healthfully in the real world. Drugs can affect the secretion of neurotransmitters, destroy neurotransmitters after they are secreted, or block neurotransmitters from acting once they are secreted. Different drugs have been developed to produce any one or a combination of these three actions to create a particular condition.

This explanation about drugs has been given because it is helpful to understand that scientists learned about the natural workings of brain chemistry in a roundabout way. As they treated heart patients, for example, they noticed that certain drugs prescribed for heart problems affected moods and sometimes caused depression. Gradually, they began to question the workings of brain chemistry, and this led to their discoveries of neurotransmitters.

Recognizing and understanding the complex interplay between the workings of your body's nervous system, your physical health, and your thoughts and emotions can give you a greater sense of control. It's really impossible for something to happen in one part of your mind or body without its affecting all of you. In fact, throughout this book, "mind/body" written as a single phrase will refer to the mind's influence on the body and the body's influence on the mind. Remember that this interrelationship is not "voodoo" at all, but something you can understand and control.

Personal mind/body checklist:

Let's review here how much you already know.
(Probably more than you think.)

Positive mind-on-body influence
1. When I think about going to a party with someone I like, I feel a rush of excitement and energy.
2. (fill in your own) _____

_____

_____

Positive body-on-mind influence
1. After an aerobics class, I have a sense of pride and accomplishment.
2. (fill in your own) _____

_____

_____

Negative mind-on-body influence
1. When my teacher calls on me, and I don't know the answer, I sweat, my heart pounds, and my stomach gets in a knot.
2. (fill in your own) _____
_____
_____

Negative body-on-mind influence
1. When I haven't had enough sleep, I'm grouchy, and it seems like nothing sinks in.
2. (fill in your own) _____
_____
_____

Perhaps now you can begin to look at the many ways in which the nervous system influences your emotions and behavior. The rest of the chapters in this book deal with subjects familiar to you. In each chapter we discuss an activity, like dance or exercise, and the mind/body connections that go with that activity. These are the connections through which you can enhance the good feelings in your life and get high — in natural ways!

2

RUNNING
AND
EXERCISING

After about a mile I get a rush and my heart starts
pumping and I feel like I have a lot of energy. If I skip
a day my body feels kind of tired.
— Sandy, student

When you're used to exercise, you get grouchy
if you don't do it.
— Mariel Hemingway, actress

I love the feeling of going fast.
— Sheila Young, Olympic skater, cyclist

Jogging is very beneficial. It's good for your legs and
your feet. It's also very good for the ground.
It makes it feel needed.
— Snoopy

The "runner's high" is not just a figment of the imagination. It's real. Researchers have linked the energetic and happy feeling (euphoria) that runners get with biochemical processes. After long, hard exercise, they say, the body ends up with extra amounts of naturally produced chemicals — neurotransmitters called **endorphins.**

Endorphins are made up of microscopic chains of amino acids that are released by the brain. They are like morphine in our blood, helping to control pain and aiding in relaxation. Unlike morphine, however, they are not harmful or addictive. They are our bodies' own anesthesia, our homegrown painkillers.

A recent endorphin study conducted at a large city hospital showed that strenuous exercise results in an upward leap in the blood endorphin level. The experiment went like this:

Doctors found seven females who were not in the habit of exercising. These young women were started on an eight-week program of working out for an hour a day. They ran and rode exercycles until they built up a good tolerance for exercise.

Each day their blood endorphin levels were measured, both before their workout and afterward. The tests showed that at first their endorphin levels rose, but only a little. Once they were conditioned, however, it was a different story. Their endorphin levels shot way up, as high as 145 percent, after the workout hour.

Dr. Daniel B. Carr, who led the experiment, concluded that the measurement "is an index of something that is happening to our brain." This may explain in part why people do not seem to notice injuries during hard exercise, why people's moods improve if they exercise regularly, and why they feel bad or listless when they stop.

Running and exercising are forms of stress on the body, but they are positive when not overdone. The body needs a certain amount of stress and use. It responds to this beneficial work with a sensation of immediate pleasure. As a result, you enjoy the activity, and feel the rewards right away.

Even before you actually begin exercising, your mind is sending messages to your body. While you are slipping into your sweatsuit or leotards or cycling shorts, your nervous and endocrine systems are gearing you up for your workout.

As you begin to exercise, your body experiences quick changes. Your heart rate and blood flow increase. Your blood pressure goes up. Your oxygen- and glucose-carrying arteries dilate, especially the ones that send blood to the muscles you're using most.

When you get into better shape, the efficiency of your cardiovascular system (heart and blood vessels) improves. Your lungs function better too. And, of course, more blood flows to the brain. Endorphins are being produced naturally, and they block any feeling of pain and boost your mood.

Here's what M.D. and jogger Thaddeus Kostrubala says in his book *The Joy of Running:*

> There's an experience of brightness and a sense of well-being. All senses, in fact, seem to respond — sight, hearing, touch, taste, smell; there is also a clarity of mind. Although there are many vivid moments, all of them are not peak ones. Different personalities have different experiences.

AEROBICS

Of all aerobic exercise, aerobic dancing is probably the most popular these days. According to Webster's dictionary, "aerobic" means "living, active, or occurring only in the presence of oxygen." When we do aerobic exercises, we exercise long enough to get the muscles to use more oxygen than they normally do. Our lung capacity is increased and the lungs expand to take in and expel more air than they normally do. The heart begins to work more efficiently, which develops more endurance for other activities. The muscles are toned, and the aerobic dancer feels a strong sense of rhythm, grace, balance, and stamina.

Aerobics dancer and author Karen Liptak says that doing aerobics makes you "feel as if you sparkle." Her book *Aerobics Basics* is a well-illustrated and easy-to-understand book for the young beginner. Ask your librarian to help you find it. You might also call your local YMCA, YWCA, or city recreation center to find out if any aerobic classes are scheduled.

There are many forms of aerobic exercise besides aerobic dance: running, jumping, and vigorous bicycling are a few. All are forms of stress, but in general, physical activity can produce a good feeling if approached with the right attitude. Find a physical activity that you enjoy and do it, three times a week, for about twenty minutes at a stretch. But *enjoy* it. Those who grit their teeth and think of exercise as a chore are creating a negative mind-on-body effect. That simply prevents the natural juices from flowing, and you miss out on the good mind/body connections — the natural highs — that exercise can set in motion.

Attitudes that will *not* help you reap the rewards of physical activity are:
— choosing an activity only because your best friends do it
— expecting *immediate* "highs"
— overdoing it, which leads to fatigue, sore muscles, and discouragement.

It's best to understand that there are no guarantees. You may not experience a "rush" at all, and what your friends enjoy will not necessarily work the same for you.

You do not have to set a timetable for yourself or break any records. You should think of what's best for you as an individual and approach your activity with moderation and common sense. Build your endurance gradually. Try to set a regular schedule if you can. It will probably result in the best overall and ongoing good feeling.

A NOTE ON
EXERCISING AWAY
MILD DEPRESSION

A team of psychologists at the University of Kansas studied if regular aerobic activity could do more than just produce an exhilarating feeling. Their study showed that the answer to their question is yes. The results were published in *Psychology Today*.

They studied forty-seven female student volunteers who were found to be mildly depressed. The students were divided into three groups:

— Group I was directed to attend an aerobics exercise class for two weekly sessions and was further directed to exercise regularly during the week.

— Group II engaged in relaxation for periods of 15-20 minutes a few times a week.

— Group III did nothing.

After ten weeks it was found that those in Group I were significantly less depressed than they had been at the start of the experiment. The conclusion was that rigorous exercise increased the production of the neurotransmitter norepinephrine, which is associated with reduced depression. (It was also believed that the friendships developed during the workouts and the goal achievements played an important role too.)

If you want to start a new exercise or sport, you might want to browse through some books first. At the end of this chapter you will find a list of suggested titles along with a description of each book.

Physical activity should be for pleasure *and* health — both to feel good at the present time and to promote a lifetime of health and fitness. By making sure that along with the exercise itself you are having fun, and perhaps expanding your social circle as well, you can make it even better. As Nicholas Kounovsky says in *The Joy of Feeling Fit*, "Anyone can turn into the 'better version of himself' he dreams of being."

SUGGESTED READING

Physical Fitness for Young Champions. Robert J. Antonacci. McGraw Hill, New York, 1962. This is a good book to assess your physical fitness, skills, and interests.

Presidential Sports Award Fitness Manual/The Total Guide. Edited by Harvey Ebel, Neil Sol, Don Bailey, and Sid Schechter. Fitcom Corporation, Havertown, PA, 1983. A thorough introduction to physical fitness, exercise, and sports. Well illustrated, with charts, graphs, and drawings.

The Joy of Running. Thaddeus Kostrubala. Pocketbooks, New York, 1978. The author takes into account physiology, the heart, metabolism, and the psychology involved in running.

The Joy of Feeling Fit. Nicholas Kounovsky. E.P. Dutton, New York, 1971. This is a fitness manual discussing the best fitness program for individual body types. Easy to understand, with illustrated instructions.

Aerobics Basics. Karen Liptak. Prentice Hall, 1983. Clear instructions, illustrations and photographs make this book easy to use.

The Young Runner. Ross Olney. Lothrop, Lee & Shepard, New York, 1978. A good background for the beginning runner. Explores equipment, running alone, marathons, and obstacles. Lists organizations and equipment sources.

Athletic Fitness: The Athlete's Guide to Training and Conditioning: Football, Baseball, Basketball, Tennis, Volleyball, Hockey, Golf, Skiing. Dewey Shurman. Atheneum, New York, 1975. A thorough and thoughtful survey for students interested in beginning a new sport.

Aerobic Dancing. Jacki Sorenson. Rawson, Wade Publishers, New York, 1981. A step-by-step, week-by-week program. Includes diagrams of dance patterns and suggests music to accompany steps. Photos and large, clear print.

3

GAMES AND COMPETITION

What kept me going was the competition.
— Grete Waitz, marathon winner

When I'm on the block, I'm very nervous and tense, but I shake out and get relaxed. When I finish a race, even if I haven't won, but have just improved my time, I'm really happy and exhilarated.
— Dara Torres, Olympic Gold Medal swimmer

It's pretty hard to describe how that feels, throwing a pass and seeing a man catch it and seeing him in the end zone and seeing the referee throw his arms up in the air, signaling a touchdown, signaling that you've just done what you set out to do. It's an incredible feeling. It's like your whole body is bursting with happiness.
— Joe Namath, *I Can't Wait Until Tomorrow.*

Try this true or false quiz:

1. Competition is normal and healthy.
True ☐ False ☐

2. Learning to compete successfully is part of development. True ☐ False ☐

3. Competition helps us with our self-esteem and self-respect. True ☐ False ☐

4. Winning is gravy. True ☐ False ☐

All of the above are true.

Winning is great, but it's not everything. Normal and healthy competition is the name of the game. The way we play it and the way we see ourselves in it can be every bit as exciting and stimulating as the end result.

We are forever competing in our everyday lives — socially, in school, on the job, for money or power. Competition on the playing field, of course, is what is most obvious to us. Man has invented sports and games of all kinds so that we can challenge one another — and ourselves — sometimes in "warlike" confrontation.

It's human nature. We compete from the time we are in the cradle, without even knowing it. We explore everything we come across from the first time we notice it; it is the same drive that pushes us to take our first steps. We don't take one awkward step, tumble, and forget it. We don't reach for a toy only once and then leave it behind. We want to master those awkward steps until we can walk and then run. We want to take the pieces of the toy and work until we fit them together. Mastering a situation gives us satisfaction, and our growing independence gives us pleasure.

As we grow older, it is natural for us to repeat what gives us pleasure. Of course we want to see a good result when we are working on something, but the way in which we achieve it seems to be as important and meaningful as the result. There is simply a lot of enjoyment in the struggle of getting there! If there weren't, we would quit early in all the "games" of our lives. We would waste away from sheer boredom.

Can you begin to see how the pleasure of such challenges in our environment is connected with self-esteem? Your active drive to compete and master helps you to feel good. Your central nervous system makes your energy available to you, and success and the excitement of exploration increase that available energy.

FIGHT OR FLIGHT

Early humans did not need hockey games or spelling bees for excitement. They had survival. When confronting an enemy, they survived either by fighting or fleeing. If they won — or escaped — they were glad to have survived.

When you face an opponent across a tennis court or a chess board, you don't have to gear up for survival, but you do gear up to win. The way early man's body reacted in a survival skirmish is exactly the way your body reacts when preparing for a contest. As you wonder "Will I win?" "Will it work?" "What shall I do?", you are unconsciously signaling part of your brain, the hypothalamus. It triggers a major set of glands, the adrenals, to produce an important hormone, the well-known adrenaline, which sends messages to your body. The adrenal glands then release more adrenaline into your blood, as well as epinephrine and norepinephrine.

You will feel good because of your achievement. Next time you face an opponent, take a minute to consider the state of your body. Are you excited? scared? perspiring? Is your heart pounding? Are your muscles tense? Try to remember that these bodily responses are actually helping you "fight."

If you are on a team, watch the body language of your teammates, too. While you are all in the locker room together, give some thought to the feelings you are sharing. In addition to the tension, excitement, and anticipation, there is the feeling of belonging, of comradeship, and of sharing a common purpose. And all these widely different feelings help to get you naturally high!

Be aware, though, that at times you may become overstimulated. Then you need to channel that extra energy or tension to work more effectively. Ways to do this are discussed later, for instance in Chapter 9, Play and Relaxation.

KILL THE UMPIRE!

Much has been written about our "killer instinct." And much has been said about sports being a good way to channel aggression. Because aggressive behavior is "allowed" on the playing field, it does release our tensions.

However, not all aspects of sports and game competition are positive. Participation in a sport should not become your only way to identify yourself: "Who am I?" "I'm a football captain." That is only a part of your identity. A person should recognize himself or herself as multifaceted, having many different and equally valuable sides. Neither should sports provoke guilt, shame, or so much stress and anxiety that these feelings follow you off the field and never leave you.

The point is that if you win, terrific! But if you don't, learn to feel a sense of satisfaction at having played and tried.

TRYING SOMETHING NEW

Often, in games and competition we see that things that are considered impossible or unattainable can be achieved. For instance, a team or a person who is clearly an underdog may come out on top as a winner. Recognizing this can stimulate us to persevere and to "try our luck"; it can also teach us to try something we have not tried before. This spirit has led to countless achievements and accomplishments. It can be!

When astronaut Neil Armstrong walked on the moon in 1965, he was realizing the dream of doing something new. His words were so appropriate: "That's one small step for a man, one giant leap for mankind," he said.

What cautious steps have you taken that have turned into a full-fledged leap? Have you ever done something that someone said was farfetched or impossible? Why, or why not?

Your personal goals

This chart is intended to help you record what it is you really enjoy doing. Fill it in and see what new and "impossible" things you may be doing, or may want to do in your life.

Complete these sentences:

I feel good when I _____

The best thing that happened to me today was _____

I think I am getting better at _____

I am continually striving to _____

Do it!

4

MUSIC
AND DANCE

When I'm at a rock concert, my heart beats so fast, I'm
afraid it's going to run out of beats and stop.
— Dori, student

Music is like a religion to me, and the more sharing that
takes place between the musicians and the audience,
the more spiritual the music becomes.
— Stevie Wonder, composer, musician

I've got to dance. That's what music does to me.
— Natalie, student

To me, dance is a total expression of myself.
— Peter Martin, New York City Ballet

Music surrounds us. We wake up to music. We drive with music playing from a tape deck or a radio, and we walk, jog, cook, and even type with a Walkman clamped over our ears.

We hum or sing or whistle while we work. We dine to music. Music makes us want to dance. Often we fall asleep to music. We are hooked. We're turned on by the beat or the rhythm or the flow of the melody. Sometimes a tune sticks in our head, and it keeps popping out on our lips hours after we've heard it. Whether it's rock, pop, blues or gospel, country, jazz or classical, everyone is turned on at one time or another by some kind of music.

While individual musicians and performers are worshipped and copied, it's their music, their message, that makes them special. There's a bond that is formed between the musicians and their eager audiences.

Music is a universal language, the language of emotions, that speaks to us in a number of ways. We use it, often without thinking about it.

For instance, it can set a mood, as when we listen to the kind of music that makes us feel romantic, nostalgic, relaxed.

In the movies music is used more deliberately. The background music tells us when a villain is coming, or when the scene is a happy one, or when we should brace ourselves for something scary or something sad.

Passion, courage, and humor can all be expressed by different kinds of music.

The singing of the national anthem at a baseball game or at the Olympics may arouse strong patriotic feelings. A stunning operatic aria, a violinist or pianist playing a brilliant cadenza, may send shivers up your spine or bring tears to your eyes. Playing in an orchestra or singing in a choir enhances our sense of power as we become part of the mighty sound. It makes us feel mighty good, too.

Sometimes music highlights memories. A particular song might remind you of a boyfriend or girlfriend you had at the time that song was popular. For an older person, it can bring back memories of an entire era in his or her life.

Today teens are more involved than ever with music and a wide variety of dance. T-shirts, albums, music videos, and record-breaking rock concerts have all heightened the music fever. For many fans, music is a language and an identity, with different groups following their favorite group's style.

This bond intensifies the effects of the music, so a performance can produce great excitement, even ecstasy. Listen to this description of a "high" for both the musicians and the audience. Writer Sam Haseyawa, in his biography of Stevie Wonder, describes one of the singer's concerts:

> The intricate rhythm of drums and congas crackled like a smouldering fire. The crowd began to tap in time to the music. Stevie's sticks flew faster over the drums. The volume swelled. And suddenly the music flared up into explosions of percussive fireworks. . . . The Music, a burning flood of emotion, rushed out, engulfing the crowd. And everyone floated on the same glowing level, held up by the energy of the sound.

Music is a powerful force, a force that increases physical energy, triggers strong emotions, and inspires passion. It can be thought of as the fuel to the mind/body connection.

WHO'S GOT RHYTHM

It's easy to think that rhythm is produced by our listening to music. But the fact is that the rhythm is already in us.

When a composer composes, he or she is expressing or echoing a form of that inner rhythm. The listeners hear it and relate it in one way or another to the rhythms which lie within themselves.

Humans are affected by patterns of rhythms and tunes. It seems a child responds to the feeling of a march or a lullaby appropriately without being directly taught their meaning.

Think for a moment about your own childhood chants when you played in a rocking chair or jumped rope. Remember the old

"*nyeh-nyeh nyeh-nyeh nyeh nyeh*"?

All kinds of words fit with this chant:

"I have more than yo-u."

"You can't ca-atch me-e." As a child, you probably heard that tune just once before you were able to pick it up and sing it perfectly, right? There is something about the rhythm of that tune — and other chants like it — that make it so catchy and universal. It echoes some common rhythm in us. And any words that are put to that tune help to make the message more powerful.

WE'VE GOT RHYTHM

The infant forming in the womb is surrounded by rhythmically moving amniotic fluid and continually hears the mother's heartbeat. Recent findings indicate that mothers feel it is most natural to carry their baby in their left arm — where the heart is — and they do this whether they are right- or left-handed. To a developing baby, life in the womb could be compared with being in an orchestra pit — in the rhythm section!

The brain, too, is in constant activity, operating and controlling our biological rhythms. We have built-in "clocks" — such as our heart and pulse beats, our sleeping and waking mechanisms, and the female's monthly menstrual cycle. There are also cycles of hormones and neurotransmitters that affect our emotions and our moods, so that it is hard to say which comes first, the music or the mood. What we do know, however, is that melody and rhythm resonate with our mind/body.

The area of the brain concerned with music is in the temporal lobes, near the hearing center. The sound travels along auditory pathways from the ear's cochlea (the inner ear) to the brain stem and into the cortex area of the brain. These are shown in the figures below. It has been established that the right side of the cerebral cortex is involved with making sense out of the music we hear.

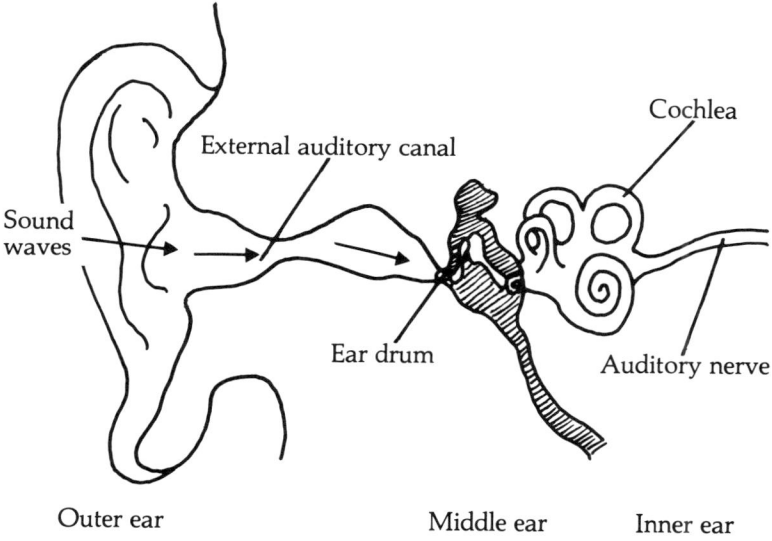

Cochlea

External auditory canal

Sound waves

Ear drum

Auditory nerve

Outer ear   Middle ear   Inner ear

A DIAGRAM OF THE EAR

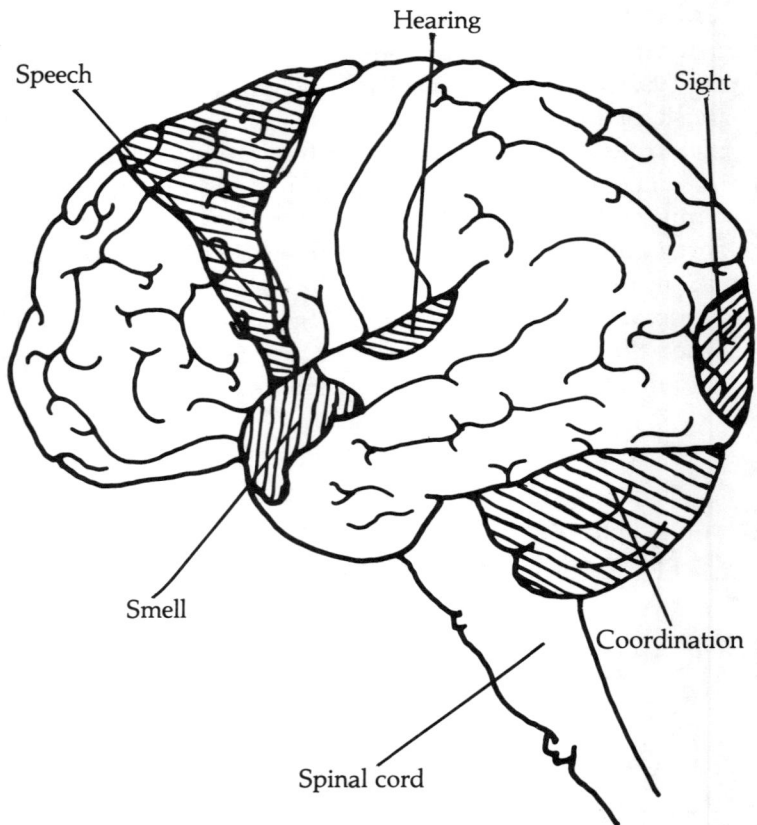

Speech

Hearing

Sight

Smell

Coordination

Spinal cord

A DIAGRAM OF THE BRAIN
SHOWING THE LOCATION OF
DIFFERENT CENTERS

As we listen, we focus our attention in a variety of ways, depending on the type of music we are hearing. A solo has little competition, so it captures our complete attention. Loud, high and vibrato notes strike the listener more often and create more impressions than soft, low and smooth notes. The hearing can be trained as well. Research shows that experienced listeners hear more than less experienced listeners.

Memory also plays an important role in listening. We are conditioned by a "brain library" of melodies we carry with us at all times, and often music is more enjoyable to us because we know what's coming next. At other times, the freshness and creativity of new music appeals to us more.

After Beethoven became totally deaf, he continued to compose great symphonies. He could do this because his musical memory was so vivid that he was able to hear music, his own music, *inside his head.*

What we hear and recall in musical experience leads to changes in our blood pressure, pulse rate, and respiratory rate. These are all part of the autonomic nervous system. Autonomic responses, of course, are vastly different from person to person, so the degree to which one person is affected will differ from another.

In addition, it has been shown that your attitude toward music can make a big difference in how you respond to it. Young people attending a rock concert can be high with excitement, while those adults who scorn rock may not be moved at all — except to scorn!

Here's what happened in a comparative study in England: Volunteers were wired as they listened to the same symphony twice. During the first listening they were asked to use their intellect to analyze the music. The second time they listened for pure enjoyment.

The results: when they listened for enjoyment, the autonomic nervous system responses were much stronger than the responses recorded the first time. Those who conducted the experiment concluded that the listeners could certainly enjoy the music while analyzing it, but their enjoyment was not as profound as when they allowed themselves to go with it freely.

In another experiment, the famous conductor Herbert von Karajan was hooked up with electrodes to instruments as he conducted Beethoven's Leonora Overture. It would be expected that his highest pulse and respiratory rates would be recorded when he was working the hardest physically, wouldn't it? Well, that was not the case. The biggest changes showed up at the places in the symphony when he felt the most emotionally charged.

WHEN WORDS FAIL US

Trying to describe music with words is difficult. A professor at Oxford University says that you cannot translate music into language any more than you can translate a picture into words. But people can try to describe how they become emotionally moved when they're listening to music or performing.

One conductor said that when he was conducting, he felt as if he were being released from his own body, and the released part rose from the stage to the rafters of the balcony.

An opera singer said that sometimes she is in such a trance when she sings that she becomes completely oblivious to the audience.

The Russian composer Aleksandr Scriabin once said that he experienced "color feelings" when the music was soft and serene, and more concrete images when the music was loud.

Tune in to some ways that can show you how music brings real highs:

— Observe yourself and others around you at a rock concert: watch the physical changes, the excitement, the breaking of barriers between people. This is getting high.

— Notice your body when you are listening to or making music. Where do you feel it? Does your heart pound? Do your eyes fill with tears? Does your skin tingle or shiver?

— Be aware of your thoughts and feelings during a slower, long program.

— Put on a record or tape, and paint or write in a free-style manner. Do you find that the music opens doors that let your imagination out?

— Participate in a song fest, join a choral group, or allow yourself to belt out a song in the shower. It's hard to feel down when the volume is up!

DANCING

To get real enjoyment from music, you don't need to win trophies or blue ribbons. Music is its own reward. And so is dancing.

Try turning on some music and see how long you can sit perfectly still, without moving a muscle, and remain feeling comfortable that way. It's hard, isn't it? Don't you want to tap your feet, snap your fingers, sway or get up and dance?

Dancing is hugging to music.

It's a sport and an exercise.

It's a permissible way to be wild.

It's a stylized mating game, a good way to flirt.

It can be an emotional release or a sexual turn-on.

You can dance slowly and dreamily with a partner.

You can dance lively with one or more partners, or alone in a crowd.

You can dance by yourself in private — with no rules and no rights or wrongs.

Dance has been an important part of every culture since man's early history. Almost every culture has celebrated important social and personal milestones with dances. Though our dances today may be less formal than some of these, they are no less of a ritual. Dance is a way of self-expression, of making contact with others, and a way of releasing tension.

Recent crazes have involved disco dancing, a flashing audio and visual experience; jazz dance, with its rhythm and tempo; and breaking, the fast-action street dancing. Terry Dunnahoo, author of *Break Dancing*, says not only does it make you feel good to get in sync with the beat, "but when you are dancing alone, YOU can be the star."

Another way to feel good is slow social dancing, where you sway rhythmically, holding a partner, with most of your attention focused on each other.

Country and folk dancing are popular in many areas of the country, and experts say that once you learn the simple basics it's easy to "kick up a storm."

Everybody has music and dance in them: their own rhythms, their own tunes, their own steps. Often we are held back from trying our own music because of the opinions of our friends and others. Yet sometimes it takes little more than grabbing a drum and banging on it for a while to get the music — and your juices — flowing.

An excellent way to express your emotions, release tension, heighten body awareness, and develop your sense of spontaneity is Creative Movement Dance. Here you can find your own harmony of mind and body.

Ideas to get you started in dance

You may feel self-conscious at first, but don't let that stop you. Remember, there are no rules, no rights or wrongs, and no one to judge you when you are alone in your room.

1. Breathe deeply and slowly.

2. Lie on your back on the floor. Close your eyes. Lift each limb, one at a time, then your legs together, then your arms, and so on. Lift your head. Be aware of your body.

3. Now do the same thing while sitting in a hard-backed chair. Roll your head slowly, forward to one side and back and to the other side.

4. With eyes closed again, stand and move about, walking with good posture, then swaying, bending, walking on your toes. Continue to be aware of your body.

5. Imagine that you are a piece of paper, a fabric like velvet or silk, a child, an animal (a cat, a deer, a frog), a symphony conductor or a rock singer.

6. Act out an emotion — happy, sad, frightened, shy, impatient, enraged, content.

7. Now imagine one of the elements — wind, fire, rain, scorching sun or a cloud — and move your body with that picture in mind.

Hopefully, you are now loose and free enough to turn on any music you are in the mood for, and enjoy your own Creative Movement Dancing.

5

LAUGHTER

I love it when you laugh so hard you start to cry
and your stomach hurts.
— Irene, student

Laughing relaxes every muscle in your body. It dispels any
negative thoughts and allows only positive ones.
— Dick Whittington, disc jockey

Laughter is therapy. It's a weapon to help you fight
disappointments and hurts. Besides, laughter
is good for your face!
— Norm Crosby, comedian

What can't you get from a druggist, but is often considered to be a wonderful medicine?

A big dose of laughter.

Author and editor Norman Cousins found that to be the case in his life. He told his story in a book, *Anatomy of an Illness,* and to audiences at the UCLA School of Medicine.

Some years ago he was diagnosed as having *peri-arteritis nodosa,* a connective tissue disease that is often fatal. Mr. Cousins explains that he had a strong will to live. An important part of his plan for self-cure was positive thinking. If negative emotions have a bad effect on the body, he reasoned, why shouldn't positive thoughts have a good effect on one's health? He listed positives: love, hope, faith confidence — and laughter.

One of his first steps was to watch Marx Brothers films. "It worked," he says in his book. "I made the joyous discovery that ten minutes of genuine belly laughter had an anesthetic effect and would give me at least two hours of painfree sleep." He watched a great many other humorous movies and read stacks of funny books.

Of course there is no scientific proof that laughter helps speed recovery, and some people ask if Mr. Cousins might not have recovered on his own. But it is something to think about. There are a number of scientists who believe that the release of the neurotransmitters serotonin and norepinephrine affect one's moods and feelings of pleasure, and may also be somehow involved in the healing process.

There have also been studies that find a direct connection between laughter and feeling good.

A psychologist at a Texas university conducted a study in which one group of students listened to a textbook reading on tape and another group listened to Steve Martin's *Wild and Crazy Guy* comedy album.

Afterward, both groups were confronted by a fellow student who made this appeal: "Say, I left home without any money today. Do you think you could spare some so I could get something to eat?"

Those who had just "been with" Steve Martin gave twice as much money collectively as the other group. Perhaps they were in a better mood. Perhaps being in a better mood can make someone more generous toward a hungry fellow student.

At a school in Pennsylvania, Patricia Ricilli and her associates, as reported in *American Health*, divided a group of students into two sections. All were told sad stories and shown slides to go with the stories, but one group was told to frown and look pained throughout the storytelling, while the others were told not to. It was reported that those who frowned were sad for a longer period of time than those who didn't frown. The conclusion was that the brain gets emotional signals from the facial muscles and skin.

Think about some of your bodily responses when you laugh:

— Sometimes we laugh until tears rolls down our cheeks.
— We jiggle and wiggle.
— We slap our knees, a friend's back, the table.
— We roll with laughter until our ribs ache (but what a pleasant ache!)

It's not surprising to find that after a good laugh, you are left with very relaxed muscles. Mr. Cousins calls laughter "inner jogging."

What wonderful things can laughter do for you?

It releases tension and anger.

It helps you cope with stress.

It allows you to act like a little kid again.

It gives you an escape hatch.

It gets you out of a tight spot.

It allows you to laugh at yourself.

It reduces the significance of a problem you might have blown out of proportion.

It frees you from always having to have a reason for everything.

It frees you from rules and manners. The Marx Brothers, for instance, are impulsive, foolish, and crazy. They spill food, jump up on tables and desks, poke fun at people, dress outlandishly. It's fun to clown around. It's fun to be outrageous now and then. Humor is play, and no one is too old for that.

Dr. Robert Maurer, Director of Behavioral Studies at Santa Monica Hospital and Assistant Clinical Professor of Medicine at UCLA, sees laughter as important in another way — as a biological need. He explains that the body needs more than just food, drink, and sleep. The body also needs attention.

One way to get attention, he points out, is to complain. ("What a killer exam that was!" will surely get a supportive response from classmates.) But Dr. Maurer says that a better way to get attention and to make a longer-lasting connection with other human beings is through humor: "Hey, want to hear a good joke?" What a good mood that can create between people!

Although you can laugh when you are all by yourself and enjoy it thoroughly, laughing with friends can lead to sharing and to feelings of belonging. Comedian and musician Victor Borge calls laughter the "shortest distance between two people." Lucille Ball says that laughing makes her feel both good and relaxed, but even better for her is making others laugh: "It's exhilarating," she explains, "I feel I have left something behind." One of her own favorite *I Love Lucy* episodes was the one in which she and Ethel went to work on an assembly line at a candy factory. When the conveyor belt sped up too fast for them to box the chocolates, all they could do was begin stuffing the candy into their clothes and then into their mouths. No one who ever saw that classic scene could forget it. One New Jersey fan does not even have to see a rerun of that show to enjoy it: "All I have to do is picture those two stuffing themselves, and it makes me laugh out loud."

Sometimes humor that is close to us or touches our lives directly strikes us deeper than a joke or slapstick comedy. A brother and sister on *The Cosby Show* are in the middle of a fight. The father enters the room. "What are you doing?" he asks. Together, without breaking off their headlocks, still grunting and groaning, they both answer, "Nothing."

Bizarre or nonsensical humor can also be based on the familiar, such as a TV scene in which Chevy Chase, Gilda Radner, and Dan Ackroyd spoof a commercial by demonstrating a spray which the announcer explains is "both a floor wax and a dessert topping."

Today comedy albums and tapes are more available than ever. Many can be rented at your local library. You can sing along with Weird Al Yankovic, chuckle over the crazy antics of Bill Cosby and Eddie Murphy, smile with recognition when you read Jim Davis' Garfield comics, or go off the deep end reading Gary Larson's cartoons in *The Far Side*.

Laughter games

You can get into the act too — after all, humor is certainly not limited to the media. There are many laughter games you can play with a small group. Try these:

1. The first person says "Ha"; the second, "Ha-Ha"; the next, "Ha-Ha-Ha", and so on.

2. Make-Me-Laff: Suggest that someone act as funny or silly as possible for sixty seconds, but try to remain stone-faced throughout. See how many seconds you *can* last. Then reverse roles.

3. Get together with some friends and improvise satirical skits. Takeoffs on TV shows are a good way to get you started with satire.

4. With a tape recorder, make up a radio interview, news, or disc jockey show. The next time your circuits are overloaded with homework and you need a good laugh break, play back your tape.

How do you feel afterward?

Another thing you can do is take an inventory of what you find really funny. List below the people, ideas, stories, or things that make you laugh. You might even try and rate them on a scale of 1 to 10, to see what makes you laugh most.

When you know what really tickles you, make use of it. Next time your're tense before a date or an exam, pick up that funny book or flick on *Family Ties* or a

What (or who) makes you laugh?

— Stand up comics _____

— Movies(Sillies/Silents/Slapsticks) _____

— Books _____

— Jokes _____

— Tickling _____

— Cartoons or comics _____

— TV situation comedies _____

— Satire _____

— Others _____

_____

M*A*S*H* rerun. Next time you're in a tight spot, put the situation in a new perspective and see if you can make light of it. Next time someone puts you down, come up with a humorous quip, or at least look for a laugh in it for yourself.

Humor is a frame of mind, a way of looking at life.

By the way, did you hear the one about. . . .

6

HAVING
A GOOD CRY

When I'm crying alone, I feel that I'm responding to
my deepest emotions — obeying them, I guess. I get
a good feeling from it because it's a true expression.
Sometimes I'm drained afterwards,
but I feel a lot better.
— Laurie, student

After a cry, I either like to take a shower or go for
a swim, and then somehow after that I really
begin to feel relieved.
— Joel, student

The basic trouble with depression is that
it's so depressing.
— Miss Piggy

You may cry over "spilled milk."

You may cry from a broken heart.

You may cry because you are furious and angry that something has gone wrong.

You may shed tears from peeling onions.

You may shed tears from an eyelash in the eye.

You may get watery eyes outside on a windy day.

Even though these tears come from the same place in your body, is it possible that they are not all made of the same stuff?

New evidence tells us they are not. It seems that the chemical composition of your tears depends on the "type" of cry you are having, on what started the tears flowing in the first place.

In the last three situations listed above, the tears were caused by eye irritants, something outside the body. In the first three situations the tears were caused by emotions.

Emotional tears and irritant tears have been found to contain different ingredients. Both contain sodium chloride and other salts, but tears shed under emotional conditions contain more protein. Some researchers believe that emotional tears also contain a type of neurotransmitter called **catecholamine.** Although there is no definite proof yet, this chemical difference could be telling us something new and important: Tears play a role in lessening emotional stress through releasing certain chemicals.

This is a very significant discovery, because in the past people often thought that tears were useless. These studies show they are not, that they have an important role to play in our lives.

Biochemist Dr. William H. Frey II of the St. Paul-Ramsey Medical Center in Minnesota believes the function of weeping is to remove toxic substances. He designed tests to study the differences between emotional tears and irritant tears. Getting tears into test tubes from volunteers exposed to freshly sliced onions was not easy, he says. But it was a lot more difficult getting people to really cry for the other part of his experiment.

After much discussion, Dr. Frey and his associates settled on showing two sad movies. One was *Brian's Song*, the story of football player Brian Piccolo's death from cancer at the age of twenty-six. The other was *All Mine to Give*, a movie about an immigrant couple settling in the wilderness, then dying and leaving a twelve-year-old son struggling to find homes for himself and five brothers and sisters.

More than half the volunteers in the study wept enough to manage to get tears into the test tubes.

Afterward, the volunteers evaluated their own moods and degree of emotion in the areas of sadness, anger, sympathy, and fear. The tears were weighed, frozen, and analyzed for content.

It was the results of this comparative test that led Dr. Frey to understand that emotional stress changes the chemical balance in a body (just as chemical balance or imbalance can change emotional stress).

Babies can release tears when their eyes are irritated. They cannot actually produce flowing emotional stress tears until they are several days or even weeks old. The reason is that the central nervous system must reach a particular stage of development before that kind of tearing is possible.

WHY DO WE CALL IT
"HAVING A GOOD CRY?"

The answer to that question might be, "Because you feel so much better after you have dried your eyes and blown your nose." Tension, anger, separation, grief — whatever it was that triggered your flow of tears — has been released. You feel cleansed. You can often see things more clearly.

Following another experiment on crying, Dr. Frey stated that 85 percent of female volunteers and 73 percent of male volunteers reported feeling much better after crying.

Sobbing, in a way, is a violent release of energy, of tension bottled up inside. Sometimes it gets so strong that you may even lose control, and not be able to stop.

Author Thomas Scheff says, "Crying is a necessary condition for removing sadness," and tears are "a necessary biological component."

Although scientists are still studying tears, it is generally agreed by psychologists that tears help relieve emotional stress. With the sadness removed or the emotional stress relieved, our bodies are less tense, our muscles more relaxed; physically we feel better, even good.

Dr. Frey draws an interesting conclusion from his study. "If crying relieves emotional stress," he says, then holding back "may increase our susceptibility to a variety of physical and psychological problems." For example, one girl held back rage and pretended she was happy and problem-free, but as a result she developed headaches.

Can you think of a time when you tried to hold back tears and then, for instance, you experienced a painful throat or developed a cold and a headache?

CRYING
IS HEALTHY

Not only do we cry when we are sad or angry, but we also cry for joy — at a wedding, when receiving a special gift that means much to us, or when greeting someone we love at the airport. This, too, is a release of heightened emotions, an expression of deep feelings, sometimes happy and sad feelings at the same time.

Can you remember a time when you felt mixed emotions, such as being happy at an older brother's or sister's marriage, yet also sad because he or she was leaving your home forever?

Crying can be personal and private. You can cry alone in your room. Or you can find yourself at a movie bursting into tears over something happening to fictional characters. You might wonder, What does that have to do with me? Perhaps something is bothering you deep inside, or you may be experiencing fear for yourself or people close to you. There might be a death scene that triggers your own fear of being in a similar situation. You may be reminded of someone you loved who has died recently. This is identifying with others.

By identifying with others, you can give vent to your own pent-up emotions. It can be a helpful means of release. For if too much sorrow or painful emotion builds up within you without your releasing it, you can end up with stress taking its toll on your body. Doctors agree that a wide variety of diseases are caused by problems in adapting to stress.

When choosing a movie or a book, you may be in the mood for being entertained. Or you may be in the mood for a real tearjerker. Pay attention to your moods. They're important signals of what you need emotionally.

Shared crying can be useful in bringing people close together. In one high school, a senior class member died in an accident. A memorial assembly was held afterward, and there was a moving photograph in the local newspaper of a group of students huddled together, crying. A classmate's death is a tragic event, but the shared crying helped the students to cope with the reality, and it bound them closer to one another at a time when they were confronted with unanswerable questions.

At the time of an illness or death, our emotions are especially strong, but we often feel helpless. Crying can take away some of that pent-up emotion. It is also a signal to others that you are in need of comfort.

"DON'T BE SUCH A CRY BABY"

Whoever said crying is only for babies and girls? Boys and men feel just as deeply as females do. Adults feel just as deeply as children.

Listen to these comments and see if you haven't heard one or more:

— She's such a good baby. She never cries.

— Don't be such a baby just because you skinned your knee. It can't hurt that much. Come on, be a brave little soldier.

— Big boys don't cry.

What's wrong with crying if you hurt or feel bad?

How good can a baby be if she doesn't cry to let someone know she's hungry or cold or tired?

Why shouldn't a man or boy release emotions through tears as easily as a woman? Is it because of our cultural upbringing? It is true that our society does not always allow men to cry. Olympic skater Scott Hamilton wept when he was presented a gold medal, but immediately he covered his eyes so the public wouldn't see his tears.

There are a few situations in which it is socially acceptable for men to cry, such as when a loved one dies.

Can you think of others? Do you think there should be more?

CURE-ALL IN A BOTTLE

We are continually bombarded by advertising which tells us that there's a magic cure to ease pain and discomfort. There are pills for this and elixirs for that. We are led to think that pain of any kind is unacceptable. The truth is, we need stress. We need challenges and frustrations, too. We can't be mellow twenty-four hours a day. Life would

---

What makes you cry?

Think back and see if you can remember the last few times that you cried. What were the situations, and how did you feel afterward? Make a list of situations in your life that are strong enough to make you cry. Here are some examples:

— End of summer camp

— Death of a grandfather

— Feeling left out at school

Now list situations in your life in which you felt like crying, but held back instead:

_____

_____

_____

---

be very dull. Pain and sorrow and moments of loneliness are part of life.

Does our society condition us to put on a happy face all the time? Maybe people who get good at hiding their emotions from others begin to hide them from themselves, too, and really don't know *what* they feel.

Emotional crying has a purpose. We should make use of it when we need to.

Some people can only cry when they are alone. Others like to have a friend nearby. Next time you feel like crying, but hold back instead because someone else is there, ask yourself why you are holding back. Is it because you are afraid of that person's opinion of you? Or that he or she might not know how to respond to you?

How do you think you would respond if a friend cried in front of you?

You might find it difficult to comfort that friend; you might imagine that he or she would have the same trouble with you and your tears. But you may be missing out on finding a good shoulder — just when you need one.

Discuss this with a friend. You may be surprised at what you both have been hiding.

7

THE EATING AND SLEEPING CONNECTION

What a strange machine man is! You fill him with bread,
wine, fish, radishes, and out of him comes
sighs, laughter, and dreams.
— Nikos Kazantzakis, author, *Zorba the Greek*

A man seldom thinks with more earnestness of
anything else than he does of his dinner.
— Samuel Johnson, writer

After a week of finals, there's nothing I look forward to
more than sacking out and sleeping in.
— Todd, student

Sleeping is no mean art: For its sake
one must stay awake all day.
— Friedrich Nietzsche, philosopher

How many times have you heard advice to balance your diet, get a good night's sleep, or take good care of your body because it's the only one you have? Bet you money you'd like to have a dollar for every time you've heard just one of those.

Well, they may be worn-out phrases, but they tell it like it is. Let's face it, without the right foods and proper sleep, it's pretty hard to feel terrific.

YOU ARE
WHAT YOU EAT

Take food, for instance. Food and the mind/body connection is something we don't bother to think about when we are devouring that hamburger with fries. But what we eat directly affects how we feel, so maybe it's worth a thought.

A man working on the Alaskan oil pipeline eats steak, eggs, and sausages for breakfast. He needs all of it for his size, his work, and for storing extra fat to burn in a cold climate.

A ballet dancer eats sliced chicken, fresh orange slices and a lettuce and tomato salad for lunch. That best fits her size, sex, and daily regimen.

Eating right is different for each individual. You need to eat according to your sex, size, and kind of activity. Eating right will make you feel at your best all the time.

The right foods give your body energy and help to build and repair it. A study at the Massachusetts Institute of Technology (MIT) showed a poor school performance and social immaturity among undernourished children. Half of these children did poorly in tasks involving memory, abstract reasoning, and verbal ability. The National Institute of Child Health and Human Development reports that poor nourishment in the key years of growth prevents a child from achieving full intellectual potential.

According to Richard Restak, M.D., in *The Brain: The Last Frontier*, "Brain function depends very much on what you've eaten for breakfast."

If you read Chapter 1, Voodoo and the Brain, you have learned about the importance of neurotransmitters — those special chemicals which allow the brain and body to communicate effectively. It turns out that some neurotransmitters are entirely dependent on what we eat. As a result, doctors in many hospitals are beginning to treat brain diseases with changes in diet.

Here are two essential neurotransmitters and some of the foods which contribute to their production in our bodies:

Serotonin: This neurotransmitter is formed with the aid of an amino acid (a protein building block) called **tryptophan.** Lab animals fed a diet high in tryptophan show a rise in their blood and brain tryptophan levels. Tryptophan is found in protein-high foods such as meat, fish, and eggs, as well as in bananas. Tryptophan is especially concentrated in cheese, milk, and turkey. Since serotonin is linked to sleep, extra tryptophan can be helpful for those who have trouble falling asleep. So that line about a warm glass of milk before bed helping a restless person become sleepy is not an old wive's tale after all, since milk contains tryptophan. Furthermore, tryptophan does not change normal sleep cycles the way drugs do.

Acetycholine: This natural brain chemical is produced with the aid of the B vitamin **choline.** Acetycholine is contained mainly in a substance known as **lecithin,** which is found in eggs, soybeans, and liver. Some researchers think acetycholine improves brain activities, including memory.

If you train yourself to eat the right foods, in the right amounts, you will increase your energy and your enjoyment of life. It's that simple — or is that simple?

CARBOHYDRATES, CHOCOLATE AND CAFFEINE

A lot of us get into the habit of craving certain kinds of foods and therefore eliminating others. When we constantly give in to these cravings we run the risk of doing our bodies harm and feeling down. If you want to feel physically well as often as possible, and throughout your life, listen to the following warnings:

Carbohydrates (sweets and starches) are an important *part* of your diet, but if you limit your diet to them or eat them in excess, your energy (blood-sugar level) will rise quickly, only to drop again in a short time. This affects the nervous system and can result in unstable emotional behavior. Recent studies tell us that the intake of too much sugar reduces the availability of chemical substances needed to produce the chemical that carries information from brain neuron to neuron.

Chocolate is a real treat for most of us. And there's probably a good explanation for why we freak out on chocolate: it's not just the delicious taste or the sugar "rush" that we like. Chocolate contains a substance that is also found in the human brain. It's called **phenylethylamine,** and it works like an amphetamine. (Chocolate contains some of the stimulant caffeine, too). Scientists have found that phenylethylamine is directly related to emotional ups and downs. There are all kinds of times when we've found ourselves "dying" for a candy bar or a hot fudge sundae. They're often related to when we're feeling blue. Next time you crave chocolate, check your mood, and see if you are feeling low.

A little indulgence (without overdoing it, of course) can pick you up. But because of the "upper" in chocolate, eating a whole lot of it might cause a "crash" to follow. So you'd be wise to keep yourself in check.

Caffeine is a chemical derived from plants. It is a stimulant, an amphetamine, that increases circulation and speeds the heart rate, and is found in coffee, cola drinks, and (as mentioned above) chocolate. It stimulates the adrenal glands to produce epinephrine, which activates the pancreas to secrete insulin. Like chocolate, it can change the blood sugar level rapidly, causing a quick unnatural high that is followed by a quick low, and resulting in unstable behavior.

A WORD ABOUT
WEIGHT-LOSS DIETS

Eating can be wonderfully satisfying, especially when you are really hungry and just devour a plateful of spaghetti smothered in cheese sauce. But sometimes the pleasure of eating can become a substitute for other things we want in life. That can cause us to put on weight and feel bad about ourselves. If you really need to lose weight — for your health and your energy (and a doctor should help you determine this, not the ads you see on TV) — be wary of fad diets. They can endanger your well-being more than your extra weight will.

There is no such thing as a magic diet. Drinking only "liquid protein" or eating nothing but grapes all day not only fails to do the weight-loss trick, it also threatens your health. Eating less fattening foods (and we all know what they are), keeping your diet balanced, and exercising are far more likely to keep excess weight off and keep you feeling good at the same time.

And don't forget how your positive thoughts and attitudes can affect your eating habits. When you reach for that extra food, ask yourself what really will make you feel better: Liking the way you look? or a second helping of ice cream with chocolate sauce and a cherry?

Your doctor can help you determine what daily calorie intake — and what *kinds* of foods — will help you maintain a natural high and lose weight, if you need to. Here's a "quick calorie check":

Hamburger: 350
Quarterpounder/cheese: 518
Chocolate milkshake: 502
Ten french fries: 155
One beef taco: 180
TV dinner/franks and beans: 550
Half of a ten-inch pizza: 485
Seven chocolate kisses: 152
One apple: 87
One banana: 127
One helping of carrot-raisin salad: 185
One cup of plain yogurt: 122
One fried chicken leg: 90
One cup of chili: 334
An egg salad sandwich: 280
One cup of skim (nonfat) milk: 88

IS THERE REALLY
A PURPOSE TO
SLEEPING?

Our bodies have many biological needs. Food and drink are the needs we think about most often. But sleep is another, equally important, need.

One of our built-in clock systems helps to regulate our twenty-four-hour cycle. In their book *Sleep*, science writer Gay Luce and psychologist and writer Julius Segal define sleep as a "progression of repeated cycles, representing different phases of brain and body activity."

Sleep gives us a chance to slow down. Our muscles relax, and oxygen is distributed to all parts of our bodies. Brain activity, body temperature, heart rate, and general alertness are all different in the morning. Hormonal changes, as well as the rhythmic rise and fall of serotonin, play a role in sleep.

Even though there have been hundreds of experiments dealing with the process of sleep, the need for sleep is still a mystery. We do know, though, that without it we suffer. (How long does it take you to "catch up" after you have stayed awake most of the night studying for finals?) We know that with it we are regenerated. Without it, we experience all kinds of distortions in our perceptions and our ability to deal with life.

Going without sleep for thirty to sixty hours can cause some very bizarre behavior. Dance marathoners of the roaring twenties, TV personalities staying up for fund-raising telethons, and lab experimenters have shown this to be true. After some seventy hours without sleep, not only is depth perception seriously disturbed, but a person is hostile and depressed and can no longer perform simple tasks. After eighty to ninety sleepless hours, hallucinations are experienced. These symptoms are not permanent and will disappear after a sleep of thirteen or fourteen hours.

In contrast, a good night's sleep involves five stages (as measured by brainwave activity tests):

1. light, drifting
2. moderately deep
3. deep

4. deepest
5. REM (rapid eye movement), a light, dreamy state of sleep in which brainwave activity increases

In the morning we awake recharged, refreshed, and reassured.

EVERYBODY DREAMS

Don't believe anyone who says he or she never dreams. Everyone does. In fact, not only does everyone dream, but dreaming is important to mental health. (Lost dreams are made up when a sleep-deprived person resumes sleeping.)

There are a number of dream periods each night, the longest one coming in the early morning hours. These dream states are characterized by rapid eye movement (REM), even though your eyelids stay shut. If you remember your dream, you've awakened during one of those REM stages. If you can't recall a thing about your dream, you've awakened from a state of non-REM sleep.

Many theories on the purpose of dreaming have been put forth, but there is no single agreed-upon answer. Dr. Ernest Hartman, director of the Sleep and Dream Lab at Boston State Hospital, believes REM dreaming helps in the learning process and also reduces stress by resolving or helping us to adjust to our daily problems.

This often happens in what are called "altered states," which can be described generally as any state when we are not in our normal "waking" consciousness. Sleeping and dreaming are both altered states; so is the condition we described as "sleep deprivation."

Another altered state is the drowsy one just before we fall asleep:it's called hypnagogic. During those moments we experience images or visions and have imaginary "conversations." Ofen we feel we are floating. Lying in the sun or floating in water can cause the same sensation.

Many of us suddenly come up with ideas or hit on a solution to a problem during the hypnagogic state. It may last for only a few minutes, but don't sell it short!

Eating right and sleeping well don't give you the immediate rush of winning a race or being asked for a date by someone you like, but they are important for you to reach those other heights. They are fundamental to keeping you fit and feeling good all the time so that you can enjoy your life to its fullest.

8

GETTING
AN IDEA,
ACCOMPLISHING
SOMETHING

Eureka, I've found it!
— Archimedes, Greek mathematician,
father of experimental science

Having a new idea for a book.
Inching along chapter by chapter.
Getting the book published.
Having another new idea for a book.
— M.E. Kerr, writer

The rush of inspiration keeps me fired and excited.
— Norman Lear, TV producer

Accomplishing something gives me this sense of
pride. It makes me like myself. I'm jubilant.
— Larry, student

The joy of moving our bodies to vibrant music, the pleasure we get from a beautiful sunset or the smell of a rose, these seem to be the first and most direct kinds of pleasures we experience. But don't forget the other kinds — the ones that start inside.

IDEAS AND CREATIVITY

When you come up with a fresh, new idea, you are making something from nothing. You are putting together fragments and forming them into a new, organized whole.

Your creative act is any form of expression that adds new pleasure and meaning to your life. Each one is different; each one is individual. Being creative does not mean you have to be a genius or the head of your class or standing front and center onstage. If you're not a Numero Uno kind of success, it doesn't mean that you're a failure. There are umpteen shades of success in between.

CHALLENGES AND ACCOMPLISHMENTS

When you are totally absorbed in something, when you have to make your way slowly and painfully over a river of sharp stones (so to speak) to get where you want to go, you're entitled to an overflowing sense of fulfillment when you arrive. After all, you did it! Your pride is a justified sense of self-worth and satisfaction in your achievement. Reap your reward and get high on it. You did it!

DISCOVERING

As children we are everything in one package — a scientist, an explorer, an adventurer. Joy for us as a youngster is everything and everywhere. As we grow, though, those small joys may begin to diminish. If once we were so delighted in our learning experiences, why don't we keep looking for new ones to replace the old?

Here are some stories told by those who have discovered the joy of new or continuing accomplishment.

ART

I worked on this painting, and oh, I just didn't know how I was going to finish it. Well, finally I did, and it was really worth doing. I realized it's one of a kind — no one else in the world can do it exactly the way I did. I felt good inside, showing it to my friends and my parents, and my friends' parents, and I liked hearing comments on my accomplishment.

Then, I didn't even know it, but my art teacher entered it in a competition, and I couldn't believe it when I won. That was my first award. When I heard my name, I felt like a queen. That's the kind of thing that's your moment! (Rona, student)

A SMALL BUILDING

I made a model city in shop, and an architect, one of the fathers at school, saw it and said, "I have two young sons at home," and he offered to pay me for it. Wow! Can you imagine how that made me feel! (Todd, student)

ACTRESS

Working, whether it's acting or working out a dance, is exhilarating to me. It's also exhausting and can make me feel spent, but in a good way. Performing in a stageplay can be physically demanding, but when I put my mind on a goal, meeting the challenge and then feeling my progress and seeing my idea fulfilled, I have a truly high sense of accomplishment. Having ideas and inspiration makes me work better. They spur me on! (Linda Purl, stage and screen actress)

GETTING A FIRST JOB

When I got the phone call telling me I was hired as a camp counselor, I was really happy. I felt as if I was worth something, and that somebody wanted me for my talents. I couldn't get over the thought that I was going to get paid for something I enjoy doing. (David, student)

IN THE KITCHEN

One time I gave a surprise party for a friend, and I baked this fabulous decorated layer cake which took me hours. Then at the big moment I carried it in the room on a round plate, and suddenly everybody went oooh and ahhhh. I just felt like I was grinning and smiling through and through. (Alice, student)

DISC JOCKEY

When I come up with an idea I get a great inner satisfaction. It can keep me bouyant and happy and up for an entire day. It's something that doesn't have to be shared and something that doesn't need outside strokes. It leaves me with a feeling I love — one of inner smiling. (Dick Whittington, radio disc jockey)

REACHING OUT

I spent hours collecting money for the Muscular Dystrophy Telethon, and when I turned it in at my local station and knew I'd gotten money for some handicapped kids, I had never felt so warm inside in my life. (Greg, student)

OUTDOORS

The best thing about rock climbing is meeting a series of small challenges that start out looking like impossible feats. It's a good feeling to use my skills and physical ability meeting those challenges.

With mountain climbing, you get this sense of airiness, and when you get to the top, it's elation. Standing up there, I know that very few others have stood on that point and seen the super view I have. (John, student, mountain and rock climber)

DANCING ON
THE SCHOOL STAGE

It comes from inside of me, an idea or a fantasy that I want to express. I express it in dance. After I choreograph it, then I can teach it to others, and it's such a good feeling to be able to do it. Something I did is important enough to share.

When I perform, it's letting go inside, allowing myself to be free and not worry about things. I'm just having a good time.

It's fantasy land. It's cloud nine. (Bridget Michelle, student)

MAGIC MOMENTS

I love those magical moments when after a lot of hard work I find that I can relax in a different situation, and that I learned things which take me further than I ever thought I could go.

I really relish that feeling of being able to let go when I'm working well. Each time I experience it, it makes the next time possible — I'm better able to resist the impulse to take the easy way out — and I'm more willing to put up with the tension and confusion, anxiety and fear of the learning process.

Somebody once said, "The other side of fear is freedom." The exciting news is this: You are in charge of that journey. (Shari Lewis, puppeteer, author, symphony conductor)

Your personal accomplishments

For one week keep a list of every idea you come up with and everything you accomplish (no matter how small you think it is) that makes you feel good. Here are some examples:

— Thought of the plot for an English class skit and wrote most of the script.

— Made fifteen out of twenty baskets in our intramural basketball game last weekend.

— Finished reading a hard history book I never thought I'd finish.

Now list your own ideas and accomplishments:

_____

_____

_____

_____
_____

Some people feel that getting an idea and making it real is the best feeling in the world. So value your ideas, and let them work for you.

9

PLAY AND RELAXATION

When I've just finished a good book I feel sated, I feel
alive, I feel gratified and rewarded and complete.
— Suzanne, student

Before I take an exam, I always do some deep breathing
and then visualize myself flying down the ski slopes,
totally in control.
— Jon, student

When the ideas fail to come, or when I want to reward
myself for a good day's work I take a leisurely bike ride
through the prettiest area I can find.
— Judy Wade, playwright

One of the best ways to feel good is to go on a vacation: ten days at an exciting ski resort, a week on an exotic beach, a luxury "Love Boat" cruise to Mexico. It's great to get away from stressful problems and have a refreshing change of scene.

Vacations and trips, however, usually require money, time off from school or work, and companionship. So you might want to consider going on a mind/body trip through relaxation and breathing techniques, meditation and visual imagery, and play.

It's free!

It's safe!

It takes very little time, and you can get almost the same effect as you do on a trip to Tahiti!

LEARN HOW TO RELAX

Your mind and your body act together. When you're worried, whether about writing a term paper or getting an after-school job, your body reacts. Your blood pressure increases. So does your heart rate, and even your breathing. Think of what you do when you are tense. Do you clench your fists and tighten your jaw? Do you grind your teeth? Hold your breath?

You will probably notice two very important things: (1) When you are tense, so are the muscles of your body. (2) When you are tense, your breathing changes. You may either hold your breath or take short, shallow ones. In either case, not enough oxygen is getting to your brain.

Learning to relax

Learning how to relax your muscles and breathe deeply can relax your mind as well. Try this relaxation technique:

Step 1

Lie down in a quiet room. Try to make yourself as comfortable as possible. Close your eyes.

Step 2

Take a deep breath and hold it for ten seconds. Slowly exhale. Do this breathing-holding-exhaling sequence four times. Let all of that stress pour right out of your body and your mind. Every time you take a breath, take peace and calmness right into your body.

Step 3

Starting at your toes, tense every muscle in your body for ten seconds, then let go and relax. Go all the way up to your eyebrows: tense — let go — relax. Let your thoughts enter your mind and flow on out again. Repeat the whole sequence if you feel you need to.

Step 4

Count slowly to twenty, and when you reach fifteen, begin counting aloud. Tell yourself that at the count of twenty-one you will open your eyes and be alert and refreshed.

———————————————————————

This will take you about ten minutes. The exercise can be done almost anywhere and you don't really need to be lying down. You can do it with others around you — for example, while riding in a car or bus or sitting and waiting on a park bench. Try doing Step 2, the breathing exercise, before starting something you find particularly stressful. Many students find that when they are very nervous during an exam, their mind goes "blank." Taking a minute to relax and breathe properly restores oxygen to the brain and brings the facts and theories you studied back to mind.

LEARN HOW TO MEDITATE

You don't need to track down a bearded guru, spend $100 to obtain a secret mantra, or retreat to a faraway commune to learn how to meditate. You can learn in less than three minutes, right now, right where you are!

Meditation is a combination of concentration and relaxation; a technique for keeping the mind peacefully thought-free. It will train you to focus on doing one and only one task at a time. This ability can be applied to many areas of your life, to help you give yourself completely to the task of the moment and accomplish your goals. The result is a wonderful feeling of control, competence, and confidence.

Meditation also has physiological effects. The mind becomes more alert and focused, but the body becomes deeply relaxed. Heart and respiration rates are lowered. Meditation produces a physiological state opposite to that produced by anger or anxiety.

As you mentally concentrate on doing one and only one thing at a time, signals sent to your physiological apparatus become simpler and more efficient. The result is healthy bodily relaxation, and more energy.

A simple meditation exercise

The following is a simple and basic meditation technique. There are other techniques too, and after you master this one, you might want to experiment with others. With any method, try to do it at about the same time and in the same place.

Step 1
Make yourself comfortable. Do some of the breathing and relaxation techniques you've already learned.

Step 2
Close your eyes. Begin to take slow, deep breaths through your nose.

Step 3
Every time you exhale, repeat the same calming word to yourself. (Good calming words are PEACE, CLEAR, and OPEN, but you may prefer others.) Continue this for about fifteen minutes: Inhale and exhale as you repeat your word. Let your mind unwind; don't think about anything. Don't even think about the word, just say it. Let your thoughts float by like lazy leaves. Don't stop to catch a leaf; just let it float past you.

Step 4
When you are finished doing the repetitions, sit quietly for a few moments before you open your eyes. Do this as often as you like.

⎯⎯⎯⎯⎯⎯⎯⎯⎯⎯⚫⎯⎯⎯⎯⎯⎯⎯⎯⎯⎯

Don't expect flashing lights or sudden insights into the meaning of the universe. Over a time you will, however, begin to feel generally more relaxed and in control of your life. This technique can also help you fall asleep.

TRY VISUAL IMAGERY

You can go on a fantasy trip in your imagination. There are many ways to go, but we'll tell you about three: with a friend, with a voice talking calmly through a tape recorder, or alone in your mind.

With a Friend
Choose someone with whom you feel safe and comfort-

able, someone whom you know quite well. On separate, small pieces of paper, write down places you both know and like, or places you would like to visit: the seashore, outer space, a cool green forest, a pleasant time or place in your memory — anywhere at all. Put these pieces of paper in a hat, then choose one and take turns guiding each other there.

While one person closes his or her eyes and sits or lies in a comfortable position, the other acts as a tour guide. Let your imagination flow — feel the water your friend is describing; smell the damp, dewy grass; taste the freshly picked strawberries.

On Tape
Read several fantasy trips, or have a friend read them into a tape recorder. Speak in a clear, well-modulated voice. Travel as above, at your leisure.

In Your Mind
Carefully choose a time or place that helps you feel peaceful and happy. Transport yourself to this "spot" whenever you need a break from routine or pressure. It's very important that on these "mind trips" you do not hurry, but stop to smell, feel, taste, and look carefully at the wondrous sights of your imagination. Use all your senses.

Bon voyage!

Choose your own meditation trip

There is no limit to the number and kinds of trips you can take in your mind, using visual imagery. You might try the one below or make some variation of it, alone or with a friend.

You are far away from home, on a clear, cool lake, drifting along on a raft. You are calm, relaxed, and serene as you lie on your back and float.

One hand skims along the water, leaving faint ripples behind.

Your hand touches a water lily, and as it does, the soft white petals of the flower begin to grow.

Near the water lily you see a large fish, glistening and shimmering in the bright sunlight.

Would you like to stay on the raft? Ride the fish? Or become enveloped in the soft, sweet-smelling petals of the flower?

If you choose to ride the fish . . .
. . . swoop through the swirling depths of the jade-green water, feel the rush of the water wash over you and cleanse and purify you. Explore the visual splendors of the aquatic world, with its irridescent turquoise fish, the pleasant pinks and oranges of the winding coral, the lazy, floating wisps of green seaweed. The water flows over you, and you are calmed by the sound of silence.

If you choose to slip inside the water lily . . .
. . . feel the velvet touch of the petals, luxuriate in their pure white beauty. Be cleansed and lulled by the deep perfume emanating from its delicate blossom. You feel safe, warm, and at peace.

If you choose to stay on the raft . . .
. . . feel yourself gently rocked by the rhythmic waves of the lake below. Count the never-ending laps of the waves until you feel yourself drifting toward tranquillity. The sun's rays warm you. The blue sky draws you upward. You are floating on a cloud and have a sensation of being a part of a spiritual world, at one with the universe.

Once you have enjoyed and experimented with this kind of guided imagery, then perhaps you — and your friends — can move on to create your own.

ALL WORK AND NO PLAY MAKES JACKIE A DULL PERSON

The previous section dealt with structured forms of relaxation, but of course you've always known how to relax without having to learn how from a book! Perhaps you've called it by a different name — PLAY. Play is not just kid stuff, but the stuff that makes human beings tick. It's the ability to have fun, to really enjoy *what* you are doing, without worrying about *how* you are doing. It's the ability to lose yourself totally in the activity of the moment. Sometimes even work can feel like play if you are absorbed enough to forget your worries.

Sometimes play is merely a change of scene or pace, like taking time off from your regular activity to see a movie, visit a friend, throw a Frisbee, or play a game of tennis. And sometimes play involves the silliness and giddiness we associate with being a child.

Whatever it is you enjoy, the hallmark of play is the sheer fun of it, combined with a feeling of involvement and a sense of physical and mental "letting go."

Scientists believe that creativity — and problem-solving — involve a mixture of play/relaxation and hard work. Have you ever had the following experience? You are unable to finish a particularly tough assignment — maybe a math problem or a story due for English class the next day. You decide to take a break, have some fun. When you return to your desk, refreshed and relaxed — Eureka! You finish the assignment easily and efficiently. Creativity is also the ability to recombine familiar concepts in new ways, and sometimes you need to "step away" from a task to see it differently. A healthy balance of hard work and play (too much play, like too much work, soon becomes tedious) helps produce a relaxed frame of mind, so that your vitality is enhanced while stress is reduced.

So give yourself permission to play. Take time off to daydream and spin fantasies for yourself. If you find that you are daydreaming while working, perhaps that's a sign that you need more time to indulge in an airy dream or two. Pay attention to the focus of the dream, perhaps taking some time to write it down. Often "wishful thinking" is an expression of a real need, and can motivate you to take action or make a plan. If the wish is not attainable (a trip to the moon, a handsome prince or princess, that pot of gold at the end of the rainbow) perhaps you can find a reasonable facsimile — a refreshing vacation, a new friend, an after-school job to earn extra pocket money.

Reading, all kinds of reading — fiction, nonfiction, newspapers, poetry, even cereal boxes — is a potentially relaxing activity too. Not only can it allow you to escape into another world and give you that refreshing "letting go" sensation, but it has another positive effect. Often the world we live in is stressful simply because it is so complex and changes so rapidly. "Getting into a good book" allows you to identify with characters who may express thoughts and ideas you couldn't find words for. This can provide direction and perhaps some meaning when things seem confusing.

There are many trips to take, and sometimes the most relaxing ones require no "traveling" at all.

10

REACHING OUT,
REACHING IN

The more good feelings you project toward people, the
more good things will come back to you.
— Lorenzo Lamas, TV actor

I can be at peace with myself sitting outside, watching,
touching, smelling, being warmed by the sun. Other times
I'd rather sit with a mug of tea and read a book.
— Clinette, student

I want to talk to someone when I'm lonely, but everyone
seems to be involved in their own things.
— Marie, exchange student

A circus owner bought a most remarkable crow. The next
night, his wife told him she had just finished cooking it.
"You cooked it?" howled the owner. "That bird could
speak eight languages!" "So," shrugged the wife,
"why didn't it say something?"
— Old Joke

LONELINESS. What does it mean to be lonely?

It may mean different things to different people.

Sometimes it means not having a special someone to trust or to love.

Or not being near the people you love.

You may feel lonely even in a crowded room.

Or you may feel that, because the telephone doesn't ring, no one wants to be with you.

Whatever loneliness is to you, the sensation is close to an aching emptiness. It is an uncomfortable feeling of isolation from others when you don't want to be isolated. It is a longing for human attachment. This feeling is one every human being has experienced. The longing is very powerful simply because being held and comforted by another human being is the first of our human experiences.

Some experts believe that a need to be close to others is built into our biological inheritance. Thousands of years ago, when primitive man traveled nomadically in packs, becoming isolated from the group often had life-threatening consequences. In other words, keeping close to familiar people or to the group was necessary for survival. Even today it's considered "dangerous" to live alone without a connection or contact. Some people believe that our longing for companionship when we are alone is as natural as our need for food and drink.

Have you ever experienced a distinct feeling of relief at seeing a familiar face in a crowd? A connection to others immediately makes you feel better. It's a primitive need.

So if you can get a drink of water to relieve your

thirst or eat a snack or dinner when you're hungry, what can you do when you are lonely?

You can seek out company.

But it's not as simple as that.

Remember the definition of loneliness — that uncomfortable feeling of isolation from others *when you don't want to be alone.*

What can prevent a lonely person from fulfilling a need for companionship? Imagine, for instance, that you are reading this while stranded on a desert island. If you feel lonely there, that would be understandable. What is more likely, though, is that you have people within talking or telephone distance. If that's true, and you nevertheless ache from loneliness, you may be kept from reaching out by your very own thoughts.

I'm not good enough.

I'm too different.

I'm shy and scared.

Nobody will like me.

They're all friends. They don't need me!

Are there other thoughts you have harbored that may have kept you from reaching out?

Often these internal, repetitive thoughts, or "ruminations," can make you so self-involved that you withdraw even further, believing you have no choice but to be alone.

REACHING OUT

It hurts to be lonely when you don't want to be. Reaching out at a time of self-doubt is difficult and takes a great deal of courage. The act of reaching out, even though it's painful at first, may serve to break the chain of negative thoughts keeping you separated from others.

Reaching out gets you "outside yourself" and helps you let go of your self-critical, anxious thoughts. Furthermore, what's hard for you may provide satisfaction because you have accomplished something challenging you set out to do.

Once, long ago, a poet, John Donne, wrote, "No man is an island." He meant that everyone in some way is a part of the world.

There are many ways to reach out. Think first of the connections already in your life, and consider how you might enhance them. There may be family members, friends, or classmates with whom you want to deepen your relationship. You might start by having some informal conversations or suggesting activities that are fun to do together — like joining a computer or nature club, attending a sports or musical event, or simply going for pizza.

You might think beyond your immediate circle and take a bigger step — into your community. Many teens find it satisfying to become involved in volunteer projects. You can help in a hospital, clinic, or foundation; coach a team of young kids or lend your services at a Y. School districts often have tutoring programs for teens to help children after school hours.

In one network of churches, teens spend a few weeks every summer building houses for needy families in poverty areas in Mexico. "Doing that kind of work gave me a new perspective about life and myself," one high school boy said. "And besides, we had fun too!"

Students in a synagogue raised money to buy food for the elderly and needy and packed and distributed it as well. "I felt I was doing something that really made a difference," a boy said. "I was helping others, and it was directly useful." A girl also working on the project added, "I felt fulfilled being part of the group."

A girl and boy helped a handicapped child in his home once a week, playing with him and aiding with his exercises. "Every time I left I felt a mountain-top high," said the girl. She also became good friends with the boy who volunteered with her.

If you have done a small service to one person, and remember your own good feeling at seeing the smile or hearing a thank you from him or her, you can imagine how your satisfaction could be multiplied by helping more.

The inner rewards are sometimes enough in themselves when you reach out to others who accept your helping hand. Often there can be additional surprises as well.

If you feel like it, you might want to take a step beyond your community and reach out into the world. You can join a political group on a local or national level, or an organization that works for world peace or for feeding the world's hungry.

Whatever you choose, the important thing to remember is that your reaching out is a personal statement. Do it in a way that enhances you, makes you feel good, and makes use of your own unique interests and capabilities.

Being involved with others allows you to let go of your personal anxieties. It can relieve boredom and give you the opportunity to have fun as well. New friends provide a sense of community and a comfort that comes from knowing that others share in your beliefs. When peers show that they accept and like you, you will begin to feel a greater self-esteem and have the stronger confidence to reach out even further.

The connections you make will also help you; sooner or later a positive contact with people brings good results.

SOME THINGS
ARE NOT WHAT
THEY APPEAR TO BE

Some people think that drugs or alcohol help them to "loosen up" and become more outgoing. Actually, they do the reverse. You may feel like the life of the party, but the party is artificial and short-lived. Drugs and alcohol do not lead to the enhancement and growth of an individual, but instead may actually stunt development as perceptions are blurred and motivations become self-centered.

What about cults? Are they physically and mentally healthy? Do they really offer the meaningful and loving life they promise?

Clergy, psychologists, sociologists, teachers, and many others speak strongly against them. Cults don't exist within the framework of the members' normal lives at home, school, or work. They involve strong ideals of devotion and dedication to a person, thing, or idea. Often they may require leaving the family, friends, school, or work, giving up all money and possessions, and living in a rigidly controlled social structure. And the conditions they impose don't necessarily promote spirituality, good works, and fellowship.

The real test of any situation or experience is what you get out of it, and some people's experiences with cults are more positive than others. Often, what members of a cult are looking for is a sense of direction, and guidance. For some of them, finding a mentor (a teacher or someone who takes the place of a teacher) or becoming close to an older friend, employer, clergyman, or other role-model can fill that need within their normal social situation. A mentor could be an older person you trust, someone you feel you can look up to and from whom you can learn. He or she may teach you specific skills, or be a lifestyle guide.

Mentors are supportive and will allow you to grow and trust yourself and your feelings and opinions. Making a healthy connecton with mentors can be satisfying in many ways for young people.

Some people find it hard to make connections on their own. Therapy, either with a qualified individual or in a supportive group has been very helpful to many people, who then begin to acquire the skills and courage to reach out on their own.

SOLITUDE —
REACHING IN

Solitude is being alone by choice and enjoying your own company. It's a time for reflection on your activities and goals. It can be a peaceful aloneness, drawing on memories, thoughts, and feelings coming from your own activities and those shared with others.

It can be a time to look into yourself. You might find that you are often pressured to act and dress and talk one way by your peers, and to live up to other expectations by your family. But it might be meaningful for you to have moments alone to think about who you really are, what you really want, and what you really like.

Do you always feel like partying with friends at a disco, dressing in similar clothes, and talking with similar phrases? There is certainly nothing wrong with this, when you genuinely feel like it.

But you might not always feel like joining the crowd. You might prefer spending an evening at home writing a short story, listening to mellower records, or putting photos in an album.

During these quiet times you can get to know yourself better.

You might enjoy a few hours at the beach:

"I am alone, but I am not lonely. I have the ocean breeze and seagulls to keep me company."
(Alice, student)

Or you might like to sit in a chapel or sanctuary:

"I like the silent prayer in the synagogue service because during that minute it shuts out everything else, like school and homework, and it makes me focus on myself and my purpose."
(Andrew, student)

"At a church retreat I went to, I got up early early in the morning both days and walked by myself in absolute quiet. It gave me time to put together some of the thoughts and meanings of what came out of our discussion groups."
(Tim, student)

"Solitude allows me to grasp my freedom and to recognize my uniqueness. I like to think thoughts I can never think in the presence of others."
(Ted, student)

"Solitude gives me time to think of things like spirituality and mystery and the unknown."
(Fernanda, foreign student)

One person might enjoy daydreaming. One might be considering summer plans. One might be thinking of a career and making decisions.

Wherever you like to be during moments of solitude, and whatever you are contemplating or imagining, those times of reflection are important to you, the inner you.

Then, after a period of restful solitude of your

choosing, you may find yourself seeking activity with others once again. A desire for company alternating with a desire for solitude is healthy and natural, just as the ocean waves reach out continuously and rhythmically between the sea and the shore.

JOURNAL-WRITING

Keeping a journal is another way to reach in toward yourself and achieve good feelings. By recording your thoughts, ideas, emotions, and experiences, not only can you alleviate loneliness, but you can watch yourself grow and change. You may begin to see patterns in your behavior and reactions to others.

A journal can be a celebration of things that make you happy, and it can also make you more thoroughly aware of the pleasurable aspects of your life. A journal is also a bit like healthy crying — a release of emotion in a safe, nonjudgmental environment. And it's fascinating to reread a journal and discover the personal themes that run through your life, and the changes you've made.

If you keep a journal, try not to make it a chore in the sense of "having to do it." You certainly do not need to *work* at it every day — approach it creatively, even playfully. Make it personal and honest; its purpose is not necessarily to be shown to others, unless you wish to. Many young people today have learned to think of a journal in a very broad sense. It may be a written record, but it can also be a scrapbook of pictures, letters, drawings, lists, stories, and mementos. It can even be your voice on tape.

One boy kept a large box which he had fun decorating in a special way: The outside of the box represented his own outer parts (photos of himself, pennants, report cards, etc.). Inside the box he kept symbols of his inner, "hidden" self — written fantasies and plans, stories, toys from childhood, a letter he had written but never mailed.

Soon he noticed with pleasure that parts of his hidden self were no longer secrets, as he gained confidence and put some plans into action. What had begun as a playful, creative activity turned into a way of becoming better acquainted with himself.

Your journal may be your art portfolio, copies of letters you never mailed to famous people, or a collection of poems. Remember, a journal can be anything you want it to be. It is a unique reflection of a unique growing individual — you.

11

LOVE

Being in love is like a bacon cheeseburger with
everything on it.
— Richard Benjamin, actor, director

When I really love someone I feel like that person is the
only person that matters. Every time I look at him my
stomach turns over. I can spend hours thinking about him
— like after we go out I think of everything he said and
every detail of what we did.
— Anna, student

I never dreamed I could ever feel this way. I'm just happy
all the time it seems, and I don't know where all this
energy is coming from. I sure do have it though. I can't
wait to get up in the morning, and I feel like talking to
people wherever I go, people I don't even know.
— Michael, student

Falling in love is a rainbow without any rain.
— Connie Samovitz, lyricist

You don't have to be told that love is a high. Some people think it's the ultimate!

Turn on your radio. It's a sure bet there's a love song playing. Love is everywhere. It makes the world go 'round. What's more, it's been that way since humankind began. It's natural to want love. We seek its joys and comforts. We need it.

Love is a different kind of high, though, from the ones that we have discussed so far. You are not as much in control as you would be when exercising, for instance.

When you find yourself in love, you find yourself a little bit out of control. After all, that's part of being in love, isn't it?

Listen to some expressions we've all heard:

I'm crazy in love.

I'm nuts about her.

I love him so much it takes my breath away.

He sure did fall hard for her.

I can hardly eat.

I'm wild about him.

Love is a thought, a feeling, an emotion. It has been said that the organ of love can be found between your ears. And your whole body can be affected by a thought or feeling about love.

Remember the talk about neurotransmitters? You'll know, then, that there is a basis for experiencing high spirits and for experiencing low spirits. Scientists understand that brain chemistry changes as a result of such a powerful emotion as romantic love.

But wait a minute. What are those expressions again? Crazy? Falling? Having your breath taken away? Isn't that all quite extreme? Well often love is at its best when it is a bit on the wild side!

Does this seem to be a different kind of situation from the others, in which you have more control and you make yourself stronger?

Love can have its weakening effect, making your knees wobble at the sight of someone special or making you wait anxiously by the telephone. But the feeling of being out of control is not an entirely bad one. It is balanced by the excitement, the anticipation of what you are going to receive from the person you love.

Love, then, leaves you strong and energetic, weak and vulnerable all at the same time. How can that be?

Well, physically this is related to the workings of your sympathetic nervous system. Your heart rate speeds up and your blood pressure rises; you're geared up for something exciting, but something that still holds a mystery, that is still unknown. You're aroused, and some part of you is even a little frightened, especially if it's your first love.

How do you feel when you're in love?

Make a short list of your *physical reactions* to being in love with or being strongly attracted to someone.

1. _____

2. _____

3. _____

4. _____

Now make a short list of your *feelings* and your emotional reactions at the time.

1. _____

2. _____

3. _____

4. _____

Now ask two friends to do the same. Compare. Chances are there will be strong similarities.

———————————————————————◣———————————————————————

Feeling very strongly attracted to another person makes us see them as someone "special." We see everything that is wonderful and exciting about that person and idealize him or her. This is the basis for romance, for the romantic love that develops between two people. For some it happens suddenly, abruptly; for others it develops gradually and unnoticed. Either way, it is probably the most powerful force known!

Romantic love, of course, is not the only kind there is. Don't forget the importance of love between parent and child, sister and brother, friend and friend, you and someone you admire. All of these kinds of love unite one human being with another. And all of these help to prepare you for falling in love, for the love that takes you out of yourself, where you want to give yourself and want most deeply to be accepted by her or him.

This brings us to an important question: What must come before you can truly love someone else?

Before you can give, you must have something you can give away.

If you reflect on your own feelings about love, you'll

discover some things about yourself. You'll find out how much of your emotional ups and downs come from your thoughts. You'll also find out that tuning in to those thoughts and feelings helps expand the concept of who you are.

You've probably already guessed the answer to the question, what must come before you can truly love someone else? You're right. It's self-love. (And self-respect, too.)

SOME COMMON IDEAS
ABOUT ROMANTIC LOVE

Puppy love, or having a crush, or infatuation. You might hear that it's not the real thing, or that it's silly. But it is just as important to young people as mature love is to adults. Remember, though, that as you grow your needs change.

Love is blind. This old phrase means that we are sometimes so dazzled by one part of a person, that we fail to see the negatives. Yes, the emotion of love can blur faults that are glaring to others. In some situations these negatives may lead to a destructive relationship. It's hard to assess such a relationship if you are involved in one, but if your intuition is telling you that you might be hurt, pay attention.

Love at first sight. You may see someone at a party, and you may experience a feeling inside so powerful that without knowing that person, you're sure you're in love. What's happening? Most likely it is attraction. The attraction may be physical, or to the magnetism and personality of the other. It may also be an attraction based on a memory of a former girlfriend or boyfriend, or on a secret cherished fantasy. The attraction is thrilling at first, but since the object of affection is still strange, the feeling is not necessarily love. Love deepens with knowing the other.

Being in love with love. It is possible to fall in love with love. You may long to have someone to hold and someone with whom you can share your life, just as people do in books, movies, and on TV. This is understandable. Fantasies are normal, but if you look for another person to fulfill your fantasy, you may be disappointed because a real flesh-and-blood person can never live up to one's romantic dreams, and such a relationship is both unrealistic and short-lived. Often it is hard to distinguish between romantic fantasies and the realities of a relationship.

LOSS OF LOVE/
LACK OF LOVE

You could also be in a relationship that you're afraid to end because you don't want to be left alone. This is understandable too.

We feel lost, empty, and disappointed when love fades or we have none at all. After a relationship ends, you may feel you will never have another one again. But the ability to love can always be revived. Although it may take time, it is likely that you will find a romantic relationship when you really want one, because your ability to love never disappears.

During the times you may be without a special someone in your life, try to remember that you have not lost your entire self. You are not without your identity. Loving and being loved are not substitutes for having an identity of your own. Love doesn't produce self-esteem, what it can do is reinforce it.

If you do feel lost and forlorn, put a little joy in your life. Remember what we said in the chapter about laughter, about the connection between your feelings and thoughts? If negative attitudes affect the body in an unpleasant way, then if your thoughts are good ones, they will have a good effect on you.

Positive thinking about yourself

Positive thinking is one of the most important skills we can learn. A good mental image of yourself can take you a long way. Try the exercises below to develop a strong positive image about yourself, one you can express to others as coming from deep inside you.

1. Study your best qualities. Picture yourself at your most likable. Practice this two or three times a day, while you're waiting for a bus, lying on a beach, staring out the window, whenever.

2. Make a list of these qualities here:

Good Stuff About Myself

_____

_____

_____

_____

_____

3. Write a letter to yourself, as if it were coming from a best friend who thinks you are terrific! Be sure to mention the qualities you listed above.

4. Now let's visualize. As if you were watching a movie in your mind, think of a time when you felt really terrific about yourself. Can you remember why? Pretend it's happening again.

You might even think of yourself as the director of your own show. Because you are!

SEXUAL LOVE

When we are responsible and mature enough to become sexually active, we are entitled to enjoy the different pleasures of sex.

The sexual orgasm is the height of ecstasy. There are many stages leading to it, starting with images in the mind or the presence of a partner, and leading to the gradual building up of sensations throughout the body.

Simple beginnings of fantasies and thoughts in the mind trigger bodily responses. So can the stimulation of erogenous zones of the body, which leads to the activation of glands which secrete hormones.

Sensations of excitement fill you. You feel perspiration, and your heart beats faster as your sexual energy flows freely. You move rhythmically without consciously thinking about it. Physiologically, muscles contract, pupils dilate, heart rate doubles, and spasms occur — all within a short time. Momentarily you surrender control.

You are charging and discharging, until you reach the height — the climax — and experience the full orgasm.

Then the orgasm is followed by a deep sense of contentment.

It's not easy to describe this height of this ecstasy, but here are some ways people have tried:

A rush.

It's like you're floating.

Waves of intense pleasure followed by relief and elation.

Impossible to describe, since there's nothing else like it in human experience.

Feels like rising into heaven from the depths of heat.

The experience of sex becomes deeper, more pleasurable, if you care for your partner in ways beyond physical attraction. It can also be made more pleasurable by first getting to know yourself, your desires, and your needs.

Some ways to develop your awareness of both your body and what feels good sexually are to study the subject of sexuality, and understand the use of fantasy, self-arousal, and masturbation.

Fantasies, or daydreams, are an important part of romance and sex. We imagine things we wish or hope and plan for, or sometimes even things we fear. We daydream about being off in the woods in the moonlight with someone to whom we're attracted: we picture ourselves being crowned prom king or queen; we daydream of being sexually involved with someone we know or perhaps a performer on the screen.

I like the fantasy where I have the female lead in a class play, and a boy I like is the male lead, and we have this scene where we kiss. But on the night of the play he takes me in his arms and kisses me for real, hard and long, and I know that he's in love with me. Whenever I imagine this, I get very excited and wish that boy who I only know a little, was really with me. (Freshman girl)

I'm always dreaming about doing things I would never do in real life, like I'm lying naked on the beach, and two girls come over, walking slow and sexy, and they take me in the water. Then I undress them and we lie on the shore and have intercourse with the waves rolling on top of us. (Junior boy)

There is no such thing as a typical fantasy or a right fantasy. Each person is unique and we imagine our own personal scenes and dramatizations. More than anything else, the "right" fantasy is the one we feel closest to, the one we like the best.

Sometimes our fantasies may seem frightening. They might be highly inappropriate to act out in real life, and too bizarre to even talk about. Generally, though, they are expressions of deeper feelings that are helping us deal with real-life fears and desires, and they don't necessarily indicate that there is anything wrong with us.

Masturbation is the act of pleasuring yourself, and is a natural and healthy way to learn about your own body. Dr. Eleanor Hamilton, in *Sex with Love*, says it's particularly useful during early adolescence as a release for sexual tension. There are many different steps over a period of time leading to fulfillment, and self-exploration is certainly one of them.

Sex education courses can be very helpful, and so can discussions in books. The more you know and explore, the better you will feel and the better you will be as a sex partner. A suggested reading list on the topic of sexuality is included at the end of this chapter.

Before you choose to become sexually active, it is important to be aware of your feelings — who you really are and what you really want. Many teens feel pressured into sexual involvement, when inside they don't feel comfortable or ready.

In several cities, discussion groups are held at YMCAs, family planning centers, churches, or synagogues in which teens express their feelings, their hesitations, and their fears. Many are learning to understand that not everyone is ready to take on the responsibility of having a sexual relationship. They recognize the need for education and information about pregnancy, about venereal diseases, about safe sex. They also discuss the need to be careful about one's own and others' feelings in this most sensitive of contacts. They are encouraged to make up their own minds instead of bending to peer pressure. After they get in touch with their truest feelings, and they decide it's best to wait, they learn to say: "I'm not comforable with this situation yet."

One boy said: "Most guys are always boasting about the sex they're into, but I decided that was them. I decided I wanted to take it slower."

A girl said: "I can understand myself and my feelings more, and I think I'm ready to make my own decisions. I know what's right for me."

Seriously consider what is right for *you*.

If you don't feel comfortable yet, it is acceptable and best for you to say so directly. You will find that when you are mature enough to accept the responsibilities and when you and your partner care about each other in special ways beyond physical attraction, your physical love will be more wonderful.

SUGGESTED READING

The Facts of Love. Alex Comfort, M.D., and Jane Comfort. Crown, New York, 1979. Well-illustrated discussion of sexuality, with an introduction for parents, urging them to engage in talk about sex with their adolescents. Especially good section on masturbation, with emphasis on the understanding that it is natural and healthy.

Sex with Love: A Guide for Young People. Eleanor Hamilton, Ph.D. Beacon Press, Boston, 1978. A frank discussion and a sound philosophy. Includes growth, anatomy, sex with safety and mutual love, and joys and pains of being with the opposite sex.

The Teenage Body Book. Kathy McCoy and Charles Wibbelsman, M.D. Wallaby Books, New York, 1978. Excellent and thorough coverage of physiology, feelings, health concerns, and sexuality. Direct and honest approach. Contains two well-researched chapters on determining when you need medical help or counseling and where to get it; help is listed state-by-state. Highly recommended.

Threshold: Straightforward Answers to Teenagers' Questions About Sex. Thomas Mintz, M.D., and Lorelie Miller Mintz. Walker and Co., New York, 1978. Short, direct answers to questions ranging from physical changes, sexual intimacy, pregnancy, and birth control, to feelings about yourself and the opposite sex.

12

HOPE

"Hope" is the thing with feathers —

That perches in the soul —

And sings the tune without the words —

And never stops — at all —

— Emily Dickinson, poet

Hope springs eternal in the human breast.
— Alexander Pope, poet

Hope must feel that the human breast
is amazingly tolerant.
— Anonymous

Hope is it! It's a true energizer!

It stimulates neurotransmitters. When the mind is full of optimism, natural recreative forces are activated. Hope stems from within you — your view of the world and of yourself.

Hope is one of life's most active forces. It offers promise and fulfillment. It expands horizons. We humans can study the past and attempt to understand and control the present, but in our relationship to the future, behind all the forecasts and statistics, the strongest force is hope.

That hope gives us the impetus to begin something new. It gives us the ability to endure something difficult. Remember our discussion about the placebo effect? Expectations and hope are the basis for those effects taking place. As Sigmund Freud said, "Expectation colored by hope and faith is an effective force with which we have to reckon."

THE POSITIVE FEEDBACK LOOP

Suppose you are a member of a football or soccer team. You've just performed, but you're uncertain about how good your performance actually was. Your coach may praise you highly for a job well done, or may tell you that you have terrific potential for showing improvement. This positive reinforcement, when sincere, can carry you a long way. You feel good receiving an encouraging word. That will feed back to your body, giving you the energy you need to do well the next time you perform.

When we talk about hope, it does not mean that we should force ourselves to have only happy thoughts to overshadow or counteract real conflicts or negative feelings. Trying to remain hopeful is not an escape; it is a way of coping with these negative feelings.

One way is to concentrate on what you can get out of the present. We all like to have things to look forward to, and we can find them in our everyday lives.

You might be expecting a special letter in the mail, or a phone call from someone you met last night. You might be getting back a term paper or school project you worked hard on.

It could be a birthday, a shopping trip, a gift you are going to give or receive; a rainy week may be ending and the sun will be out again, warm and strong; a sunny day may be giving way to a stormy night and you can't wait to curl up with a good book.

Looking forward is saving the dessert for last.

Hope involves making plans. You make plans for a party, for your classes next semester, for a summer job, or for a career. That inner hope provides the fuel you need for taking action to make those plans happen.

You might say that HOPE SPRINGS ETERNAL

because HOPE SPRINGS INTERNAL

Most of the time you are not aware of that power and control within you. You don't usually pay attention to the fact that it is there and acts as a constant source of both physical and mental action.

Once you recognize your inner hope and control as a dynamic force, you can go even further when you make plans to achieve something.

If a first plan doesn't work out, be aware of your inner resources and use them. Understand that if you had the energy and drive to make one plan, you can make another. In other words, if Plan A fails, try Plan B.

— One girl wants to become a lawyer. She researches

it and finds that the field is overcrowded. She could take the give-it-up road, or look for other connection options instead. She could choose a more specialized area of law or plan to begin a career in a smaller town for a few years. If she is really determined to enter the law field, she will find a way.

— A high school boy learned that a girl he had been dating for a year wanted to break up with him. After the breakup he felt low and lost for weeks, and most of the time he felt that he never wanted to go out again. But he had an inner spark of hope, which kept him from complete despair. Once he responded to that inner spark, he was able to spend some time during those difficult weeks after the breakup focusing on himself, reevaluating his feelings and his needs. That period of being low and lost was not wasted and meaningless. During that time he grew as a person. Five months later he met another girl with whom he began to share new interests. You can do the same, if you have faith in yourself and hope for the future. Don't give in to disappointment. Look for the option that you *can* plug in to.

— You may not get the lead in a play, but you can take a different path and work behind the scenes. You could find a new interest or talent. You could make a new friend.

— A big picnic you arranged for your club may have been rained out, leaving you disappointed. You might make last-minute arrangements with a small group to picnic indoors, make fudge and listen to music, becoming closer to some of the club members you didn't know very well.

— There might be a divorce in your family, and you could be missing the security and comforts of living with both parents at the same time. In the new situation your dad might be living elsewhere and your mother might be working full-time. While divorce can be difficult and uprooting, needing adjustment and understanding, you can learn to come to terms with it. Often, the children of divorced parents find that they learn to fend for themselves more, and develop new skills. They also gain a greater degree of independence.

Of course, there might be times when you feel that all hope is lost. If those feelings go on for too long, it could be a signal that your goals and expectations ought to be changed. Just like our thoughts and behavior, goals and expectations can be changed. We have the choice and the ability to make those changes.

POWER AND HOPE

Some doctors think that when someone is diagnosed as being clinically depressed, the depression is often from a sense of hopelessness or powerlessness, a feeling of a loss of control. When you are depressed, you lose interest in life and you don't feel like doing anything.

By contrast, renewed hope and feelings of having some power can lift a person out of depression.

What kind of power do we mean?

It is not the kind where you need to put down others or the kind that requires you to be on top or in command. It is not the kind where you feed on the constant admiration and adulation of other people.

Often we think that being popular, like a football captain, homecoming queen, or class president, is the most powerful and desirable position to be in. We envy others in those roles and long for them ourselves. Certainly there is a rush, a high, in winning a class vote or riding atop a float in a parade, but few of us will experience a lasting high from the admiration of throngs of other people. (In fact, the best leaders are not in their positions because they want to have followers, but because they believe in themselves and in what they are doing.)

That brings us to the kind of power that is meant here — the kind that comes from believing in yourself, having confidence and a healthy self-esteem. It takes power to be a regular team member, to follow, or to offer help or even to ask for it. When you recognize this, you have reached a higher level of maturity and inner power.

COURAGE AND HOPE

Growing up takes courage.

What kind of courage is meant here?

It is the ability to do something important that you don't really want to do, but know you must. This doesn't necessarily mean jumping out of an airplane with a parachute.

It means things like changing schools or moving to a new city and meeting new people or taking a harder class that will be a greater challenge to you.

It means taking a risk that can lead to something better for you.

The more you experience doing something that appears difficult to you, the easier it gets, and the better you feel about yourself.

Being a human being does not mean standing still or escaping. It means moving forward. Courage takes you there.

Now that you have read this book, you have become aware of the wide range of inner resources you have:

the strength and vitality of your body

the expressive power of your laughter and your tears

the charm of the music within you

the deepening effect of your spiritual longings

the healing ability to maintain a healthy balance through relaxation, food, and sleep

the unifying force of giving and receiving love

the courage and hope to believe in your uniqueness

As a human being, yours is the opportunity to use these natural inner resources, and meet the challenges of growing up in this exciting and wonderful world.

Use This Handy Order Form
for Your *SPECIAL DISCOUNT*
on Hunter House
Family & Health Books

PMS: PREMENSTRUAL SYNDROME An Infobook for TEENAGE WOMEN, Their Friends and Families by Gilda Berger. The first need is proper information, and this book will help young women through their encounters with PMS.
Soft Cover   96 pages $6.95

HELPING YOUR CHILD SUCCEED AFTER DIVORCE by Florence Bienenfeld, Ph.D.
A guide for divorcing parents who want — and need — to make this time as safe as possible for their children. Filled with practical strategies for resolving conflicts.
Soft Cover   256 pages   Illustrated $9.95

WATER CHILD by Judith Bolinger and Jane English.
Poems from a pregnant year, photographic images from nature. A fusion of meditative poetry with visual metaphors.
Soft Cover   64 pages   Illustrated $6.95

RAISING EACH OTHER: A Book for Parents and Teens by Jeanne Brondino and the Parent/Teen Book Group. Honest talk from both generations about freedom, privacy, trust, responsibility, drugs, drinking, sex, other vital issues.
Soft Cover   128 pages $7.95

ONCE A MONTH by Katharina Dalton, M.D.
The first book — and still the best — to explain clearly the symptoms, effects and complete treatment of Premenstrual Syndrome. By the acknowledged pioneer in the field.
Soft Cover   256 pages   2nd Edition $8.45

CHARTING YOUR WAY THRU' PMS by Virginia M. Fontana et. al.
A woman's health book and planning guide. Charting your menstrual symptoms is the *only* reliable way to diagnose PMS, and this book helps you do it.
Soft Cover   64 pages   Illustrated $2.95

GETTING HIGH IN NATURAL WAYS An Infobook for Young People of All Ages by Nancy Levinson and Joanne Rocklin, Ph.D. Being high is a natural state — *and we don't need drugs to get there.* A vitally important book for our times.
Soft Cover   112 pages $6.95

DRINKING PROBLEMS = FAMILY PROBLEMS by Marie-Louise Meyer, R.N.
The problem drinker affects all those around him. This book discusses the choices that must be made, the changes to carry through to regain control of your life.
Hard Cover   256 pages $12.95

EXCLUSIVELY FEMALE: A Nutrition Guide for Better Menstrual Health by Linda Ojeda, Ph.D. Nutrition and diet can help relieve the symptoms of premenstrual syndrome and other causes of menstrual discomfort. Includes a nutrient guide for adult women.
Soft Cover   160 pages $5.95

MENOPAUSE WITHOUT MEDICINE by Linda Ojeda, Ph.D.
Preparing for a healthy menopause can never begin too early. Ojeda's natural approach focuses on nutrition, physical conditioning, beauty care, and psychological health.
Soft Cover   288 pages $9.95

NOT ANOTHER DIET BOOK: A Right-Brain Program for Successful Weight Management by Bobbe Sommer, Ph.D. Right brain techniques to gain control of your weight, self-image, *and* your life. Includes a six-week program to obtain and maintain the desired weight.
Hard Cover   256 pages $15.95

Prices Subject to Change Without Notice
See Over for Ordering and Discounts

Add postage and handling at $1.50 for one book and $0.50 for every additional book. Please allow 6 to 8 weeks for delivery.

PLEASE PRINT:

Name _____

Street/Number _____

City/State _____ Zip _____

PLEASE SEND ME:

PMS INFOBOOK	_____ @ $ 6.95	_____
HELPING YOUR CHILD SUCCEED	_____ @ $ 9.95	_____
WATERCHILD	_____ @ $ 6.95	_____
ONCE A MONTH	_____ @ $ 8.45	_____
CHARTING YOUR WAY	_____ @ $ 2.95	_____
Pack of 10	_____ @ $25.00	_____
GETTING HIGH IN NATURAL WAYS	_____ @ $ 6.95	_____
DRINKING PROBLEMS = FAMILY PROBLEMS	_____ @ $12.95	_____
EXCLUSIVELY FEMALE	_____ @ $ 5.95	_____
MENOPAUSE WITHOUT MEDICINE	_____ @ $ 9.95	_____
NOT ANOTHER DIET BOOK	_____ @ $15.95	_____
RAISING EACH OTHER	_____ @ $ 7.95	_____

TOTAL $_____

DISCOUNT AT _____ % **LESS** $(_____)

TOTAL COST OF BOOKS $_____

Shipping & Handling $_____

California Residents add 6% Sales Tax $_____

TOTAL AMOUNT ENCLOSED $_____

☐ **Money Orders** ☐ **Check**

☐ **Check here to receive our catalog of books**

Please complete and mail to:
HUNTER HOUSE INC., PUBLISHERS
PO Box 1302, Claremont, CA 91711, USA

If you don't use this offer — give it to a friend!